The World is Confused, but God is in Control

Donald DeMarco

En Route Books and Media, LLC
Saint Louis, MO

En Route Books and Media, LLC
5705 Rhodes Avenue
St. Louis, MO 63109

Contact us at contactus@enroutebooksandmedia.com

Cover Credit: Sebastian Mahfood
Copyright 2024 Donald DeMarco

ISBN-13: 979-8-88870-270-3
Library of Congress Control Number: 2024950656

All rights reserved. No part of this book may be reproduced, stored in a retrieval system, or transmitted in any form, or by any means, electronic, mechanical, photocopying, or otherwise, without the prior written permission of the author.

Dedication

Ad Deum qui laetificat juventutem meam

Acknowledgement

First and foremost, I thank Sebastian Mahfood, publisher extraordinaire, for his encouragement without which this book would never bask in the light of day. I would also like to thank the editors of *The Catholic Register, The Wanderer, Catholic Exchange, and Legatus* for publishing, in various forms, some of the chapters contained in *The World is Confused, but God is in Control.*

Epigraphs

"In the past, and even to this day, there have been so many programs promising 'healing' for the world and proclaiming the arrival of 'true' justice in men's dealings with one another. But none of these can be regarded as complete unless it is linked with the justification before God—which is the main foundation of all justice."

- Saint John Paul II, Sign of Contradiction

"I have been driven many times upon my knees by the overwhelming conviction that I had nowhere else to go. My own wisdom and that of all about me seemed insufficient for that day."

- Abraham Lincoln

Table of Contents

Introduction 1

Section 1: The World in Confusion 3

What Is Wrong with Secular Humanism? 5
Is Education Possible in a Secular World? 10
In Praise of Folly 15
Toward an Unencumbered Life 20
Seinfeld, Stoicism, and Sanctity 25

Section 2: Catholicism in Crisis 31

Conforming to the World under the Guise of Being Christian 33
Being Catholic and the Problem of Shame 38
The Importance of Understanding the Word "Our" 43
Let Danger Have Its Way 48
Pope Benedict XVI Meets Fidel Castro 53

Section 3: The Importance of Life 59

The Heart Is a Lonely Hunter 61
Life is not a Playground 66
Baseball is not Life 71
Football and the Pro-Life Movement 76

St. Thomas Aquinas on the Abortion Issue 81

Section 4: The Path of the Christian 87

Where Is My Authentic Place?.....................89
Blessings in Perspective................................93
The Freedom to be Reasonable...................98
Four Things to Consider before Making a Proper Choice... 103
Jacques Maritain and the Apparition at La Salette: A Postscript 108

Section 5: The Blessings of Common Sense 115

Listening to the Word of God 117
Heaven is not of This World 122
Is Catholicism a Religion-in-Progress?................... 127
Mother Angelica vs. Charles Darwin 132
America Needs Help from Above 137

Section 6: God is in Control... 143

Yes, God Was Right, There Are Two Different Sexes 145
What is the Mother of All Virtues? 150
Why Is Humility so Difficult to Achieve? 155
In Praise of Domesticity... 160
Does a Career Make a Woman Hard?..................... 165

Introduction

To say that the world is confused fails to convey the depth of the confusion. The root of the confusion is a loss of a sense of God. But the problem goes further than that. The secular world displays a hostility toward the Deity. A person can be fined for reciting certain passages from the Bible. Churches are vandalized in great numbers, and the violation of the Ten Commandments is more common than their adherence. Truth is politically incorrect, marriage is foundering, and sexual identity is left to children as young as 4 years of age to determine.

Such confusion, however, is not a normal state, and conforming to the ways of the secular world does not bring peace. God is the only stable and abiding presence. Only in terms of a relationship with Him can a person experience lasting peace. The words of Christ are most comforting: "And behold, I am with you always, and to the end of the world" (Matthew 28:20). The words of Isaiah also bring us comfort: "Fear not, for I am with you; be not dismayed, for I am your God; I will strengthen you, I will help you, I will uphold you with my righteous right hand" (41:10).

There are two words in Greek that refer to the world. One is *gaia* which refers to the created world which is good. The other is *aion*, referring to the era or the spirit of the age. This is the "world" for which Christ would not pray (John 17:9-23).

We have an important, though underused, ally in reason. It is through this universal human faculty that we can recognize nonsense for what it is. Despite being surrounded by confusion, the intellect and the capacity to reason remain undefiled in their essence. Despite being underused and opposed by a wayward world, reason can spring back to life and exert its proper function.

This book encourages the reader to find God and to employ reason so that he is not enslaved by the temper of the times.

Donald DeMarco
November 5, 2024
Waterloo, Ontario

Section 1

The World in Confusion

What Is Wrong with Secular Humanism?

Secular humanism is the dominant philosophy of our time. It is of critical importance to us, therefore, to understand the meaning of this phrase so that we are not taken in by its allure. On the surface, each of the two words seem harmless enough. "Secular" refers to the world in which we live. It centers on the here and now. It is inescapable. "Humanism" refers to who we are as human beings. It is eminently realistic. And yet, these two apparently innocuous terms, when put together, form a philosophy of life that is, paradoxically, highly injurious to any human being living in the world today.

First, the term "humanism" is ambiguous. It refers to what we know about the human being in its immediacy, how the human being is circumscribed by science. But it also refers to the human being in its totality, which includes its spirituality and its relationship with God. One of the tenets of humanism in the first sense asserts that the nature of the universe depicted by modern science makes unacceptable any supernatural or cosmic guarantees of human values. Simply stated, man is on his own. He is an orphan in an alien world. In the second sense of the word, it refers to man's relationship with his creator, that morality and the meaning of life are not invented but discovered. He is at home in the cosmos.

It is written that, "Man does not live by bread alone" (Matthew 4:4). In the Lord's Prayer, the expression, "Give us this day our daily bread" refers to the Eucharist and not the bread that can be purchased at a grocery store. Bread from the earth satisfies the body but cannot satisfy the soul. The fundamental defect of atheistic communism lies in its incapability of accommodating the human spirit. There is more to the human being than meets the eye.

Aristotle, the author of *Ethics*, a work of perennial value, maintained that to offer man only what is strictly human is to betray him and to wish him ill. In this regard, what Aristotle maintains on this point is in harmony with Christianity. Marx, Freud, Sartre, Comte, and many other thinkers held that man is a complete entity solely in his earthly form.

In his book, *True Humanism*, Jacques Maritain asserts that, "There is nothing man desires more than a heroic life: there is nothing less common to men then heroism." This discrepancy is largely attributable to the fact that the latter is more difficult. As G K. Chesterton has commented, "The Christian ideal has not been tried and found wanting. It has been found difficult; and left untried."

Since the dawn of the Renaissance, the Western world has passed progressively from a Christian philosophy of life toward a form of humanism that is essentially atheistic. The appeal of atheistic humanism is twofold. First, it is undemanding. One is left free to do as he wills. This freedom is attractive to those who want to live by their senses and indulge their appetites or immediate gratification. In addition, in the absence of God, there is no final judgment. Man can sin with impunity. Self-absorption leads to self-ruination.

The disseminators of atheistic humanism can arrive under the guise of helpmates. Betty Friedan, a signer of the second *Humanist Manifesto,* wrote her best-seller, *The Feminine Mystique*, to liberate housewives. But her overriding motive was to indoctrinate them with her brand of humanism. Accordingly, she states that, "Women of orthodox Catholic or Jewish origin do not easily break through the housewife image; it is enshrined in the canons of their religion, in the assumptions of their own and their husbands' childhoods, and in their church's dogmatic definitions of marriage and motherhood." Friedan has effectively stigmatized the "housewife" with indelible ink.

The Beatles, the world's most beloved rock group, arrived as boyish and playful entertainers, but they were also dispensing humanistic messages. For example, in their song, *Eleanor Rigby,* after describing a Christian funeral, intoned the words, "No one was saved." Harvey Cox, of the Harvard Divinity School produced *The Secular City* which promoted a stripped-down Christianity. "We do not speak to him [our neighbor] about God," he wrote, "by trying to make him religious, on the contrary, by encouraging him to come fully of age, putting away childish things." Among the "childish things," as he made clear, were many of the traditional beliefs and practices of Christianity.

Politicians, no matter what Party claims their allegiance, are fearful of making any reference to the supernatural. They end up promising what they cannot produce, a utopia on earth. Secular humanism dominates their language. Historian James Hitchcock in his study, *What Is Secular Humanism*, gives credit to the mass media for the rapid of spread secular humanism in our age. Under its influence, he states, "traditional moral values were ridiculed, assaulted, and ground into dust."

In his well-researched book, *The Drama of Atheist Humanism*. Henri De Lubac, S. J, commends Fedor Dostoevsky for putting in a nutshell one important social truth: "Man cannot organise the world for himself without God; without God he can only organize the world *against man*. Exclusive humanism is inhuman humanism."

The dividing factor that separates secular humanism from a humanism that honors the spirit of the human being is *truth*. In Jacques Maritain's terms, it is the truth of man that separates *anthropocentric humanism* from *theocentric humanism*. The former, he contends, is *"the tragedy of humanism."*

Is Education Possible in a Secular World?

Education in today's secular climate has become largely the indoctrination of ideas that happen to be fashionable at the moment. It is the very opposite of what education should be. The word "education" means to draw from within. This is how Plato understood the meaning of the term. Education is a process of drawing out from the student something that is already in him. This is the antithesis of "seduction" which is imposing something alien on the student that is wholly outside of him.

Education in the best sense, teaches a person who he is. Reading, writing, and arithmetic are secondary. Civilization demands a society of people who are not confused about what it means to be a human being. Today, confusion reigns.

In the early days of university education in America, schools chose mottoes that reflected their commitments to eternal values. Therefore, the motto of Harvard was *Veritas,* for Yale it was *Lux et Veritas,* for UCLA it was *Fiat Lux,* for Brown University it was *In Deo Speramus*, for Johns Hopkins it was *Ver-*

itas Vos Liberabit, and so forth. A commitment to enduring values safeguarded education from being by seduced by the Zeitgeist. Today's schools have become a haven of division to the point that some leading universities have cancelled commencement exercises because student protests have become dangerous and out of hand.

The importance of a good education cannot be overemphasized. In the trenchant phrase of H. G. Wells, "Human history becomes more and more a race between education and catastrophe."

I had the pleasure several years ago of meeting Mortimer Adler, one of the truly outstanding American educators. He signed my copy of his book, *How to Read a Book,* and was pleased to note that its tattered dust jacket and dog-eared pages indicated a thorough reading. The book makes reference to one of the major mistakes that was (and still is) circulating through higher education--the false notion of liberalism. Adler explains how false liberalism is really the enemy of a truly liberal education. According to false liberalism, authority is tyranny, truth is unattainable, and all opinions are equal. Adler, who has a gift for clarity, points out that we are free *through* reason, not *from* reason.

Adler, whose enthusiasm for education is boundless, kindly gave me a copy of a recent work of his, *The Paideia Proposal* (1982) which outlines a more holistic and democratic approach to education. The word *Paideia* is derived from the Greek, *pais, paidos,* referring to the upbringing of a child. In an extended sense, it is the equivalent of the Latin *humanitas* signifying the general learning that should be the possession of all human beings. Adler's mind is encyclopedic and finds much value in studying contributions from antiquity.

It is interesting to note that in 1817 Thomas Jefferson proposed that there should be three years of schooling for all children in the state of Virginia, at the public's expense. At the same time, he advocated dividing the children into those destined for labor and those destined for learning. *The Paideia Proposal* takes an entirely different approach: "The best education for the best is the best education for all." Adler maintains that "There are no unteachable children. There are only schools and teachers and parents who fail to teach them." The author is, in a sense, both egalitarian as well as democratic.

An essential theme in the Paideia Proposal is that education should have two fundamental goals in view. One is to equip the student with the means to earn a good living for himself. The other, is to enable the student to lead good human life. Education in virtue, therefore, is an indispensable part of education.

Without being unduly critical of Adler's approach to education, a Christian will realize that something most important has been omitted. Earning a living and living well are unassailable ideals. What is left out, however, is how to understand who the individual person is in himself. This omission perfectly justifies the existence of Catholic schooling.

A person may have a good job and be a virtuous individual, but does he really know who he is? Catholic schools, being true to their mission, should, above all, instruct their students that their supreme teacher us not their classroom teacher, but Christ. In the words of Saint John Paul II, Christ is "the Teacher who reveals God to man and man to himself, the Teacher who saves, sanctifies, and guides, who lives, who speaks, rouses, moves, redressed, forgives, and goes with us day by day on the path of history, the Teacher who comes and will come in glory."

The God who created us dwells within us. Christ, the Teacher, draws Himself out from his student. Becoming more Christ-like is the highest form of education, one we do not expect from secular schools, but do expect from those that are Catholic. Christ reveals the truth about man and man's life and his destiny. Hence, the importance of daily prayer.

We are not mere individuals, nor are we simply members of the state. We are not mere animals, nor are we mere spirits. Christ, our Teacher is our model, one who allows our identity to develop, but in a manner in His image. As St. Paul exclaims, "It is no longer I who live but Christ who lives in me" (Galatians 2:20). And yet, Paul was fully alive. The ultimate goal of education, then, is to render man both Christ-like and fully alive.

In Praise of Folly

What should I say to a young woman who enters my classroom wearing a t-shirt that reads: "I am a Proud Member of the Pro-choice Generation?" Perhaps my response should be relegated to the realm of the imagination, which neither offends nor upsets. Furthermore, I owe it to my other students to avoid a distracting scene. Also, there might not be time after class since I must hurry to another building to begin a lecture of logic.

The word that catches my attention is "generation." It is a most intriguing fact that she owes her existence to a long line of generations that stretches back to her primal parents. From one generation to another parents said "yes" to a subsequent generation. It was an unbroken series of "yeses" that made it possible for her to be here. It is a phenomenon so extraordinary that, in the words of the immortal poet, John Keats, "doth tease us out of thought." This is something that one can be proud of and something for which the only proper response is gratitude.

Barbara Eden, star of "I Dream of Jennie," traces her ancestry back to Benjamin Franklin. Oscar winning actor, Tom Hanks is a descendent of Nancy Hanks, the mother of Abraham Lincoln. And crooner Pat Boone is a descendent of the famous wilderness explorer, Daniel Boone. Here is something about which this trio of celebrities can be justly proud. One generation salutes previous generations for maintaining a lifeline that brings them into being. It is a pride that honors a succession of generations that consistently honors the value of life. When God said, "Let there be light," He was offering a preliminary to "Let there be life."

So many generations were required to inaugurate the life of my student. How much she owed to the past! Nonetheless, seemingly unaware of the contributions of her ancestors, my student is expressing pride for the option of *not* continuing life. What is greater than life? Could it possibly be "choice?" "Choose choice," abortion zealots cry. But mere, disembodied choice is an abstraction. It has no solidity. It is a chimera!

Now, if we choose something real, such as life, we get choice "thrown in." C. S. Lewis has told us to

"Aim at Heaven and you will get Earth 'thrown in': aim at Earth and you will get neither." And he is right! If our life is circumscribed by the physical world in which we are placed, nothing, neither love, nor joy, nor beauty, nor goodness, will make any sense. Everything would be washed away with death. But when we include the light of Heaven, everything begins to make sense. Similarly, G. K. Chesterton stated that when we separate the supernatural from the natural, we get the "unnatural." It is the supernatural that irradiates the natural to give it its value. We do not fully understand the son unless we know something about the father.

When we choose life, we get arms and legs, heart and lungs, and choice "thrown in." It's a good bargain. Choice does not exist by itself. It is certainly nothing that conveys pride. It is fatuous to be "pro-choice."

There is no need for a "pro-choice" movement since we already have choice. It is our birthright. It is ours to use, morally or immorally, properly or improperly. On the other hand, we do need a "pro-life" movement because life is under attack. By the same token we need a movement that promotes justice, fairness, decency, and other worthy causes. We do not need a "pro-leg" movement because we already have legs. We already have the capacity to choose and that is a permanent part of our being.

Has my student pondered the consequences of her mother being as enthusiastic about abortion as she is? Can a person be pro-choice retroactively? Can one be indifferent to the choices of his ancestors? Can I not express my thanks to all the members of my long line of ancestors who made my own life a possibility? To what extent are pro-choice advocates banishing gratitude from the world? There was no pro-choice movement in her mother's time. Does that suggest she was unenlightened? A being that does not exist cannot express gratitude.

Pride is a double-edged sword. We can have pride in our children, our country, and our church. In this case pride honors something that is good. But we can have a different kind of pride when we encourage mothers to destroy their offspring. This is the kind of pride that is a Deadly Sin, the kind the scripture says its possessor is doomed to suffer a fall. Pride in this sense must fall because there is nothing to hold it up. We must be careful where we place our pride.

"Lord, what fools these mortals be," wrote Shakespeare in *A Midsummer Night's Dream* (Act III, scene 2). The phrase has broad application. Erasmus made use of it in his satire, *In Praise of Folly*. Being proud of promoting death is, to assert at the least, a rather foolish, if not malevolent. Let us stay with the word "foolish." It is a bit kinder. I hope my student learns something in my class that is not foolish. I am respectful of Alexander Pope's famous warning: "Fools rush in where angels fear to tread." This is a problem for everyone who wears the mantle of the teacher. Was I being angelic by not rushing in? No doubt there are times when discretion is the better part of valor.

Toward an Unencumbered Life

David Welday III, who is the President of HIGHER LIFE Publishing and Marketing, has posted an article entitled, "We Need To Live Our Lives Unencumbered." In our affluent, acquisitive age many of us have accumulated things that were once eye-catching, but now have become clutter. Welday takes pleasure in sending the possessions he no longer needs to Good Will where one's trash is transformed into another's treasure.

The notion of an unencumbered life is perfectly legitimate as long as what is encumbering is the assortment of junk that has become a burden in a person's life. When the idea of being unencumbered covers one's life in general, a serious problem arises. Should a person's life be so smooth and unburdened that it offers nothing at all that is cumbersome?

To celebrate the Harris-Walz ticket, Planned Parenthood has offered free abortions and free vasectomies during the time of the Democratic National convention. According to the *Washington Post*, "Attendees at the Democratic National Convention in

Chicago will have the opportunity to get a free abortion or vasectomy just blocks away from the event—and vasectomy appointments are filling up fast." Planned Parenthood Great River made it known that all of the appointments have been filled, but people should "check back again soon—we will share the interest form again if we have cancellations." PP has begun a waiting list. Also in attendance was "Americans for Contraception." The group plans to erect an enormous 18-foot-tall inflatable IUD which will go by the name, "Freeda Womb," which, oddly enough, is more pertinent to abortion.

The extravagant and shameless celebration by the Democratic Party of contraception, abortion, and vasectomies emerges from a background philosophy that needs to be brought to the surface. The late Rev. Richard Neuhaus once declared that Canadians have traded Christianity in for the "unencumbered life." What Father Neuhaus meant goes far beyond getting rid of mere clutter. He was addressing the enlargement of the unencumbered life to include those encumbrances that are necessary for a moral existence.

And leading the parade of encumbrances is Christianity that atavistic religion that requires its adherents to pick up the Cross on a daily basis

Behind the Democratic Party is a truly malevolent philosophy dressed up as a new and more complete sexual revolution. But the malevolence is not entirely hidden, it is peeping through at the edges. Let us prevent birth both before and during intercourse and if life persists, then do away with it through abortion. In one sense, the vasectomy is more sinister than abortion. Abortion destroys one life; a vasectomy prevents an untold number of lives.

Does the Democratic Part know anything about the rudiments of life? Life presents to everyone inescapable encumbrances, obstacles, difficulties, and challenges. They exist to rouse us from dormancy, to energies us, to vitalize us, to build character. Democrats can dance around the Golden Calf and welcome a Utopia that will never be. Meanwhile, they will be wasting their lives, rejecting any encumbrance that interferes with their somnolence.

The great Spanish philosopher, Ortega y Gasset has put the matter nicely: "All life *is the struggle, the effort to be itself.* The difficulties which I meet with in order to realise my existence are precisely what awakens and mobilises my activities, my capacities. If my body was not a weight to me, I should not be able to walk."

An image once appeared the *New Worker* depicting a young man in a wheelchair. The caption states, "Of course he can walk, but thank God he doesn't have to." To live is to be active, to welcome challenges because they help us to realize who we are. An athlete will realize how good he is only is he competes against strong opposition. Our rivals can bring out the best in us. Without rising to a challenge, a person remains a "nobody." The Democratic Party is truly tending toward a group of nobodies.

Motherhood and fatherhood are great challenges, but also are immensely rewarding. In addition, they are also necessary for the continuance of the human race. It is not the encumbrances that we must banish, but the notion that we must get rid of them.

It is a tragic fact of life that people of little character, those who have never surmounted an encumbrance, are easy to exploit. "Free" is an enticing word, though it often comes at a great cost. It is often the bait covering the hook. People will choose things that are free whether or not they need them. No doubt, some will be seduced by the siren call of "free abortions and vasectomies." Esau obtained a bowl of pottage and all he had to give up was his birthright.

Sex and politics make for a bad marriage. Sex is personal, politics is public. Sex is between two. Politics involves the multitude. Marriage is for life. Politicians are for a term. Marriage requires a vow. Politicians require a vote. Marriage demands love. Politicians crave admiration. The Democratic Party has overstepped its boundaries.

It is no longer a conjecture. The Democratic Party is clearly both the Party of Death and the Party of Lost Opportunity. Is our power to procreate a gift from God or is it a mere encumbrance that politicians should help us abolish? It has been said that democracy gives people what they deserve. But, we may ask, does anyone deserve this?

Seinfeld, Stoicism, and Sanctity

Jerry Seinfeld continues to be in the news, but this time in the unlikely role as a student of philosophy. He has been reading Marcus Aurelius, as he recently informed a journalist, an activity which has been helped him to understand the impermanence of everything and everyone we know, and the futility of fretting about things we cannot change.

The resumé of Marcus Aurelius is most impressive. He was a philosopher, an author, an emperor, and, with his wife, Faustina, a father of 14 children. He was the last of the Five Good Emperors of Rome. His reign (161-180 AD) marked the end of a period of internal tranquility. *Meditations*, his most influential book, is the cornerstone of stoic philosophy. It offers common sense aphorisms intended to help people achieve peace of mind and self-control. Among these we find the following: "The first rule is to keep an untroubled spirit." "Very little is needed to make a happy life; it is all within yourself in your way of thinking." "You have power over your mind - not outside events. Realize this, and you will find strength." "Reject your sense of injury and the injury itself disappears." The good emperor was concerned about self-control, but not sanctity.

Seinfeld wholeheartedly agrees with the emperor's philosopher. Fretting about things you cannot control is futile. "You should focus on what you are doing," he says, "get better at what you are doing. Everything else is a waste of time."

Jerry Seinfeld is an exceedingly talented human being. He is far more than a comedian. He has the uncanny knack of looking over what most people overlook. He is a man of rare insight. Yet, he could find a better philosophical tutor than Marcus Aurelius. Stoicism is not an easy philosophy to put into practice. Furthermore, it is self-centered and accords powers of self-control that appear unrealistic. Of the emperor's 14 children, 9 passed away before he died at age 58. Surely, the deaths of these children must have shaken him. Aurelius does offer the option of suicide, however, if things get out of control.

Stoicism has been criticized for wrapping its disciples in a cocoon of self-centeredness and ignoring the problems of the world. It appears to lack a commitment to social justice while proposing an iron clad self-discipline that is unrealizable. Concerning pain, a typical stoic response was: *Si longus levis; si gravis brevis* (if it is long, it will be light; if it is grave, it will be brief). Always think on the bright side.

From a Christian perspective, stoicism is not the road to sanctity. Yet, stoicism and Christianity have something in common. They are equally opposed to worrying. As we are advised in *Philippians* 4:6-7: "Don't fret or worry. Instead of worrying, pray. Let petitions and praises shape your worries into prayers, letting God know your concerns. Before you know it, a sense of God's wholeness, everything coming together for good, will come and settle you down. It's wonderful what happens when Christ displaces worry at the center of your life."

The salient difference between stoicism and Christianity is prayer. The *Meditations* of Marcus Aurelius dispenses with the need for prayer, which is tantamount to dispensing with the need for God. It responds to a philosophical problem that is universal, namely, how should we deal with things we cannot control. The stoic attempt is to shut them out; the Christian is concerned about them, but appeals his case to God through prayer. Saint Padre Pio has given us a simple phrase that has become very popular: "Pray, hope, and don't worry." God, not us, is in control of the universe. Prayer is infinitely more effective than worry. The stoics were right, but did not go far enough. Hearing the words of Jerry Seinfeld one may feel the same way. A good start, but there are wiser philosophers who offer a more complete philosophy that you may be ignoring. Please do not allow Marcus Aurelius to be your final philosopher.

"Do not fear [anything]," Isaiah writes (41:10, "for I am with you; Do not be afraid, for I am your God. I will strengthen you, be assured I will help you; I will certainly take hold of you with My righteous right hand [a hand of justice, of power, of victory, of salvation]." Both the Old and the New Testaments are advising us to trust more in God than in ourselves. In order to accept this advice, we must overcome the pride of taking care of business all by ourselves. Worry never solved a problem. There are problems that we can solve on our own. But there are problems beyond our reach that we cannot solve. Then, in calling upon God through prayer, we obviate the need to worry, an activity that is designed to end in frustration.

The way to peace is not through worry but through prayer. This attitude allows us to be concerned about the troubles of the world without useless worrying or despairing. As Padre Pio points out, prayer brings about hope. We put the things we cannot control into the hands of God and stop worrying. And then we are the recipients of peace and hope.

Existential anxiety is a common malaise in a world without God. Viktor Frankl speaks of the "existential vacuum" that people experience when they find no meaning in life. They become desperate when they realize that their worrying is in vain. Yes, as Seinfeld reminds us, we should focus on doing a better job of what we are doing. But stoicism is not the answer for members of the medical profession, to take but one example, who must be profoundly concerned about their patients. Their skills should be complemented by their prayers. The same can be said of everyone's relationship with his neighbor. We should add to our concerns not our worries, but our prayers.

Section 2

Catholicism in Crisis

Conforming to the World under the Guise of Being Christian

Sociologist Gordon Allport, in his book, *The Nature of Prejudice,* recalls a disturbing lesson he heard at school when he was twelve years old. A student asked the priest whether it is permissible to boycott Jewish stores. The priest wanted to put the student's conscience at ease. "Although God wants us to love all fellow men," he said, "He does not say that we should not love some of them more than others. Therefore, it is all right to love Poles more than Jews and to patronize Polish businesses only."

It is true that Christ did not say that we should not love some people more than others, but neither did He say that that we should love some people more than others. The priest was putting ideas in the mind of Christ that were inconsistent with his message. Furthermore, he slyly translated "people" into ethnic groups. Surely, Christ did not imply that certain ethnic groups are less deserving of love than others.

Whether or not the priest was aware of the dire implications inherent in what he was saying, the plain truth is that he was conforming to the world, in particular, by accepting the prevailing prejudice against Jewish people. Allport was hard on him: "The priest was a pious fraud, twisting religion to fit secular prejudice and planting seeds of bigotry that could, and did, grow out of hand in plunder and pogroms." When the camel gets its nose in the tent, soon, its whole body is in the tent.

A lesser love, for the priest, would be no love at all. It would be like saying to the Jewish merchants, "We love you, but we don't mind helping to drive you into bankruptcy." The issue that the priest centered on should have been *justice* rather than love. The basis of prejudice is injustice. Justice is less manipulable than love. If the student's question were phrased, "Is it okay to be unjust to your neighbor," the answer would be a resounding 'NO'."

Politics can weigh heavily on the minds of Christians. To be a Christian demands integrity. They live *in* the world, though they are not *of* the world. As another priest, Gerard Manley Hopkins, S. J., reminds us, "The world is too much with us." Therefore, Christians are engulfed by the world and become prey to any number of its deficiencies. Integrity is a lofty ideal but is nonetheless required of every Christian.

How easy it has been for Christian churches of various denominations to accept secular imperatives that are alien to their fundamental purposes. Thus, they allow room for abortion, euthanasia, same-sex marriage, and the rainbow banner representing the LGBT+ consortium. All this is rationalized in the name of being "liberal." Such accommodations, however, ultimately lead to self-destruction. A truer meaning of being liberal is freedom from the clutches of the secular world.

Oftentimes, Christians are more fearful of being called extremists, than developing the courage to maintain their integrity. Had the priest, in Allport's story, stated that it is wrong to boycott stores simply because they are operated by Jewish people, he would have been at odds with the prevailing secular climate. He may deserve additional condemnation, however, if he thought he could pull the wool over the eyes of his young students. He had attempted the impossible: the get off the hook, please the world, and at the same time, maintain his status as a good Christian.

He failed, both as a priest and as a teacher. Unfortunately, his attitude, unlike that of the vast majority of his colleagues of the cloth, could help to establish a prejudice against all priests. One bad apple can spoil the barrel.

It is a terrible thing to take Christianity, which thoroughly opposes prejudice, and use it as a tool to promote prejudice. A single compromise with the secular world can reap great havoc. Thus, the supreme importance of integrity. Let us not give the enemy a foothold. One can bleed to death from a single puncture.

In 2 Timothy 4:3-4, St. Paul speaks of people becoming deaf to the Word of God and seduced by the allurements of the world: "For the time is coming when people will not endure sound teaching, but having itching ears they will accumulate for themselves teachers to suit their own passions, and will turn away from listening to the truth and wander off into myths." Paul has a special advisory concerning those in a teaching profession who misrepresent the truth of the Gospel. At the same time, he warns students about their "itching ears." Institutions of higher education carry no guarantee that what they teach constitutes education.

Our misguided teacher, whom Allport cites, opens a broad discussion both on the prevalence of prejudice, but also how people who should know better can easily deceive their students. The Gospel does not deceive. The lesson of the Good Samaritan places one's *neighbor* above class distinction, a factor that can serve as a basis for prejudice. The parable refers to a Jewish priest and a Levite who passed by a man lying by the side of the road who had been robbed, beaten, and left half dead. It was the Samaritan, for whom class distinction meant little, who came to his aid (Luke 10: 25-37). We are all neighbors to each other. Christ never taught that some neighbors are worthy of more love than others. Love and neighbor are both irreducible categories.

Being Catholic and the Problem of Shame

There are many reasons that justify a sense of shame: possessing stolen goods, lying to your friends, cheating at cards, taking credit for something you did not do, dishonoring you parents, and the list goes on. But there is one reason not to feel shame, and that is being a Catholic.

However, there are false reasons for attaching shame to being a Catholic. It is important to spell these out so that their flimsiness becomes more apparent and less credible. The first is that being a Catholic is to belong to a minority. 20% of Americans are Catholic, but how many of them are true Catholics? The majority is said to rule, but there is nothing in being a member of a majority that makes one superior. "The majority is always wrong," said the Norwegian playwright, Henrik Ibsen. The majority can be complacent, dominating, and narrow minded. There is nothing inherent in being a member of a majority that justifies looking down on others. Furthermore, the majority is unstable. The pagan majority in ancient Rome gave way to a wave of Christians.

Secondly, Catholics seem odd because they believe in things that are said to be unbelievable. We think of Christ being present in the Eucharist, the Mystical Body, The Holy Trinity, the Virgin Birth, miracles, and the act of forgiveness. Human history, however, is filled with episodes of the unbelievable passing into not only the believable, but the acceptable. The atom, lighter than aircraft, flying to the moon, supersonic speed, the existence of microbes, recording human voices, and countless other phenomena were all considered at one time or another to be unbelievable. But, all these un-beliefs quietly passed into everyday life because some courageous and enterprising members of a minority brought them into being.

In 1 Corinthians, 4:10. St. Paul proclaims that, "We are fools for Christ, but you are wise in Christ." In the eyes of the world, Catholics, indeed, can appear to be rather foolish. They are unselfish, would die for a friend, and when they are assaulted, they turn the other cheek. Their actions and the way of life can make them a laughingstock. And yet, ridicule from the secular world means little to them as long as they are *with* Christ. Their day of exoneration will come. They have triumph in their pocket.

Being part of a minority, professing what seems to be unbelievable, and suffering scorn and ridicule from the secular world need not cause shame if one is a true Catholic. Shame is a sign that there is some deficiency in one's faith.

Another factor that brings about a sense of shame is that Catholics claim that what they profess is the truth. This does not set well in a world where relativism prevails and is the dominant philosophy. Is it not an act of pride to assert that one's belief is true? Is it not better to keep an open mind and not presume that one is right? It is not a matter of pride or hubris, however, to declare that one knows truth. The mind is made for the reception of truth, just as the eye is made for color. Even if one believes in higher truths, those that God has revealed, this should not be an occasion for pride. A Catholic who believes in the truths of his faith must assume an attitude of humility. Truth does not belong to him as a private possession but is given to him to share with others. Therefore, the Catholic, rather than feeling any sense of pride, should be grateful that he has been given truth that he is obliged to share with others. His claim to know truth should be accompanied by the virtues of humility, gratitude, and generosity. In this light, a Catholic should feel honored to be a Catholic.

There is another temptation for the Catholic to feel shame. It is the sense that he is left out. Catholics are woefully under-represented in elite colleges and universities, and also in high positions of government. Although Catholics do make important contributions in every field of endeavor, it is true that Catholics will need to overcome obstacles that do not block the career paths of many non-Catholics.

The August 14, 2024, edition of *The Catholic Report* addresses the question whether we are living in a "No Catholics Allowed Society." Author Thomas M. Doran believes that "For all intents and purposes, no Catholic perspectives, themes, or ideas are welcome. Increasingly, such perspectives are shamed." A true Catholic will be pro-life, pro-God, pro-family, and pro-traditional marriage. But he is placed in a world that is pro-abortion, pro-gender change, pro-euthanasia, and pro-same sex marriage. Doran concludes that the "*No Catholics Allowed* threat is more worthy of Catholics' attention and commitment than climate change because a *No Catholics Allowed* worldview degrades the human spirit and human culture."

Shame induces inertia. It destroys incentive. The problems that Catholics face in today's world should arouse Catholics rather than immobilize them. The situation will worsen if action is not taken. The true Catholic is not bigoted or misogynistic or homophobic. He should not allow slander to be its victim. Rather, he should find confidence in his alliance with Christ and work against seemingly invincible odds to renew the face of the earth. It is a might job but one well suited to the real Catholic.

The Importance of Understanding the Word "Our"

When His disciples came to Him and asked how they should pray, Jesus instructed them to say what is commonly known as "The Lord's Prayer." The first two words, "Our Father," convey a significance that is central to our relationship with God. It not only addresses God as the receiver of our prayer, but also establishes both our primary relationship with Him as well as our relationship with others.

God is our *Father*. As Father, in the highest sense of the word, God is both creator and protector. At the same time, He is a model for all biological fathers. But he is *our* father, the possessive pronoun indicating all people. He is not simply *my* God, but God to everyone. We are His children. Therefore, our prayer should commence with a sense of humility. This also means that we are all related to each other as brothers and sisters. The word *our* is both intimate and inclusive.

When Christ uses the term *our*, He includes Himself. He unites Himself with us in praying to *our* Father who is also His father. Our prayer, then, is united with Christ's prayer, both directed to the ultimate Father who is in heaven. Here we find the humility of Christ. We are all children to the heavenly Father.

In our post-Christian world, there are feeble attempts to imitate the first two words of the Lord's Prayer. The promotion of inclusivity aims at bringing everyone together. But this noble effort is without a foundation. It is promoted by will and nothing more. The "Our Father" tells us that we are all included as God's children. Therefore, the real basis for this inclusivity is God as *our* Father. In this case the unity of all people has a real foundation which is the reality of God. Unlike inclusivity, which is a proud ideology, praying to God as children demands appropriate humility.

The word *our* may be elusive in that it can designate possession or merely being something larger than ourselves. Latin, which is a superlative language for grammatical precision, distinguishes the possessive from the partitive genitives. When we speak of "our house" we use the term *our* in the possessive sense. We own the house. It is legally ours. It does not belong to anyone else. But when we say "this is our country" we do not infer that we own or possess it, but that we are merely part of it. Here, we use the partitive genitive. If I say, "This is my wife," I am not inferring possession, but alluding to the fact that I am part of the marriage.

There is another use of the word *our* which denotes intimacy. When a couple states, ecstatically, "They're playing *our* song," they are referring to how that particular music is part of their romance, how it has brought together in the past, how it is an important part of their lives. The same can be said about, our favorite restaurant, our favorite movie, our favorite haunt, and so on. This personal use of the word *our* is perfectly legitimate. However, it by no means suggests that they own the various things that helped to solidify their relationship. The same song can be any other couple's favorite song.

Now, we move into a more profound notion of the term *our* when husband and wife, let us say, procreate a child. Both the mother and the father have contributed equal amounts of DNA. They are equally parents and equally responsible for the upbringing of the child. In this case, the word *our*, as in the expression "this is *our* baby," has a far deeper meaning than when it is applied to *our* house or to *our* favorite song. And yet, in so stating, it refers to stewardship rather than ownership. Nonetheless, there is something quite profound about proclaiming that "this is *our* baby. It is a high point in the declaration that something is ours.

We are reluctant to part with the many trifles we own such as a book, a compact disc, a painting, a teapot, etc. Materialism is usually accompanied by the selfish desire to hang on to things long after they have exhausted their usefulness. These are things for which the possessive pronoun *our* can be applied. The child of parents, however, despite being *our* child, is commonly given up by abortion. What did all those expressions of what is *ours* really mean when the summit of what is more truly ours was destroyed?

The things to which a husband and wife assign the word *our* in a limited way (our income, our home, our car, our cat) are but a prelude to the culminating point when they can say, "this is *our* baby." Abortion contradicts all the previous indications of a relationship (to which the word *our* is testimony). The time arrives after husband and wife have accumulated all the things that they can say are *ours* when the momentous decision must be made: "What should we do with *our* unborn child?"

In the Day of Judgment, God will ask us how we used the freedom of choice that was ours to utilize. Our freedom can be a frightening thing. Through freedom we can either win or lose our souls. Did we exercise our freedom so that our choices were also God's choices for us when we prayed together to "Our Father"?

Let Danger Have Its Way

It is common knowledge that the Chinese radical for "crisis" means danger + opportunity. It is widely assumed that danger and opportunity move in opposite directions. I think there can be a third possibility: the opportunity to bring danger to the catastrophe against which danger alone is simply a warning.

There appears to be clear evidence that a catastrophe has been achieved at The Australian Catholic University. On October 21, 2024, Joe de Bruyn delivered the commencement address to the graduating class at The Australian Catholic University. Mr. de Bruyn was a former president of Shop, Distributive and Allied Employees Association. He served for more than 20 years on the Board of Campion College in Sydney Australia. He presented his keynote speech after being given an honorary doctorate at ACU.

After the severe backlash to Harrison Butker's orthodox address at Benedictine College in Acheson, Kansas, Catholic commencement speakers have been forewarned. It is a most dangerous thing to present traditional Catholic views to allegedly Catholic students at a Catholic school. Presumably, the world has changed, and Catholicism has given way to Liberalism.

Prior to his address, Mr. de Bruyn had been asked to change certain passages in his speech. He did not comply, stating, "I thought about that, and I thought that they have asked me to give a grad speech so I'm not going to be censored by them as to what I can and cannot say."

Nonetheless, his address triggered, if not a riot, a virtual mass exodus. What did he say that that sent hundreds of graduates rushing toward the exit? He dared to point out that abortion kills 80 thousand unborn babies a year in Australia and approximately 42 million annually throughout the world. Added to this figure are the countless human embryos destroyed through In Vitro Fertilization. He cited the fact that God instituted marriage, according to *Genesis,* as the union of a man and a woman. He emphasized the point by stating that "every society on Earth at all times" has recognized marriage in this sense.

Well, this was too much for the grads to bear. A student by the name of Charlie Pantelli got up and started the exodus. He estimated that 95% of the people in attendance left with him. The remaining 5%

were filming the event because they felt that what was being said was so outlandish that the news of the fiasco should get out.

The school, in sympathy with the offended students, offered counselling for them. What could be more soul traumatizing than graduates from a Catholic School listening to a Catholic speaker presenting a Catholic speech? Perhaps the counselling should have been made available for the real Catholics who had witnessed what for them was a catastrophe.

Not surprisingly, de Bruyn did not backtrack, according to a news report. And why would he? Petulant students walking out in protest to an essentially innocuous talk does not constitute a compelling argument for changing one's religion.

The hostile reaction may have been puzzling for Joe de Bruyn. "I was in the position where I had been invited by the university to give a graduation speech in my capacity as a Catholic layman coming to Australia Catholic University for an award, an honour, for my services to the Catholic Church, so it was most appropriate for me to deal with Catholic issues."

What the media reported was not so puzzling. The world has always been at war with the Church. It characterized de Bruyn's address as "an inappropriate, self-indulgent rant about issues of life and human sexuality that had little relevance to a graduation ceremony."

But this was hardly the case. De Bruyn was trying to help students of Catholic faith to live in the world. According to Sydney's *Catholic Weekly*, he told the graduates that, for more than 40 years, he had worked in a union that covered warehousing, retail and fast-food companies, fighting for the rights and wages of some of the lowest paid workers in the country." Why should this part of Catholic teaching be acceptable while issues involving marriage, and life and death not be? Catholicism is not a pick and choose religion. It has both harmony and integrity. Why was this important feature of Catholicism not made known within the classrooms of The Australian Catholic University? The entire text of de Bruyn's speech is available in *Catholic Weekly*.

His concluding comment may not have been heard by the fugitives, but it is clearly unassailable as well as most appropriate for a graduating class. *"As happened to me, you will be faced with issues in your professional and personal lives where the general opinion of the majority of the population is at odds with the teaching of the church.*

"The world is too much with us," as Gerard Manly Hopkins once said. Catholics can be absorbed by the world and tone deaf to the very religion to which they claim to belong. The Liberalism of the world is enslaving. It fails to apply the brakes when brakes are needed. As a morality without restraint, it ceases to be a morality at all. Freedom without restrain is freedom run amok, better known as chaos. In order to maintain its value, freedom must be placed under the guardianship of reason. Reason intervenes long before freedom threatens to invite a catastrophe. A Catholic is a sign of contradiction, not an eager pawn. What message will the graduates of ACU bring to the world? They cannot run away from everything!

Pope Benedict XVI Meets Fidel Castro

One cannot imagine two more disparate characters meeting and being cordial to each other than Pope Benedict XVI and Fidel Castro. The former being a pious and highly educated leader of the Catholic Church; the latter being a Marxist-Lenin socialist whose administration oversaw human rights abuses. Nonetheless, no matter how different, human beings are human beings and have that as their common denominator.

The meeting took place on March of 2012 in Havana. Pope Benedict XVI offers a brief account of their rendezvous in his book, *Benedict XVI: Last Testament.* The pontiff was in his last full year as leader of the Catholic Church, while Castro was 85 and ailing. The pope's impression of Castro was that he had not "yet come out of the thought-structures by which he became powerful." The word "yet," however, contained a glimmer of hope because the president of Cuba (from 1976-2008) had seen through "the convulsions in world history" and was pleased that "the religious question is being posed afresh."

The former dictator of Cuba asked Benedict XVI to send him some literature. Was Castro merely being diplomatic or was he genuinely interested in Christianity? We, of course, will never know, but his request remains intriguing. At any rate, Benedict XVI send him a copy of his 1970 book, *Introduction to Christianity*, a most appropriate work for this occasion. The Holy Father did not consider Castro the type of person who would be likely to undergo a "major conversion," but believed that since he was keenly aware that so much has gone wrong, he was prepared to look at things in a different way.

Pope Benedict XVI is not naïve. He understands how extremely difficult it is for a Christian and a hardened atheist to engage in productive dialogue. He begins *Introduction to Philosophy* by citing another thinker who shared this view, *Søren Kierkegaard*. The distinguished Danish existentialist was fond of using parables to impart his philosophy. One of his parables features a clown who was already dressed and made-up for his performance. A fire broke out in the circus and the manager dispatched the clown to go into the village and get help for there was a real danger that the fire would quickly spread and engulf the village itself. The villagers, however, mistook the clown as and advertising agent for the circus. The more the clown pleaded with the villagers the harder they laughed. Given his clown costume, he had no credibility. They thought he was playing his part splendidly until it was too late for help and the village was burned to the ground. "I think that's just how the world will come to an end," said Kierkegaard, "to general applause from wits who believe it's a joke." For Pope Benedict XVI as well as Kierkegaard, Christianity is no joke. But how can it be communicated? How can it protect itself against gross misinterpretation?

In the clown parable, the clown cannot communicate with the villagers. The result is disaster. The villagers fail to recognize their commonality with the clown. A Jewish parable makes the same point. Martin Buber tells the story of a non-believer who paid a visit to a very learned Rabbi. His intent was to convince the Rabbi, through argumentation, of the reasonableness of atheism. When he arrived at the Rabbi's home, he found his would-be adversary walking up and down with a book in his hand, wrapped in thought. Suddenly he stopped, looked at his new arrival and said, "But perhaps it is true after all." The doubter opposed the Rabbi with all his strength, but the "perhaps" echoed back at him and broke his resistance. There is a "perhaps" in all of us.

Benedict XVI comments on this parable by stating that "both the believer and the unbeliever share, each in his own way, doubt *and* belief, if they do not hide away from themselves and from the truth of their being." Neither can entirely escape from either doubt or belief. The believer has his doubts, and the doubter cannot rid himself of the temptation to believe. If Castro read the first 21 pages of *Introduction to Christianity,* he could have found Pope Benedict XVI to be his brother and a meaningful dialogue could ensue. The pontiff was Joseph Cardinal Ratzinger when he authored the book. As he reiterates, "Just as the believer knows himself to be constantly threatened by unbelief, which he must experience as a continual temptation, so for the unbeliever faith remains a temptation and a threat to his apparently permanently closed world."

St. Thérèse of Lisieux grew up in a thoroughly religious atmosphere. Yet, this saint, who was virtually cocooned in religious security, had troubling temptations to unbelief: "I am assailed by the worst temptations of atheism," she acknowledged. On the other hand, famous novelist William Somerset Maugham lived as a confirmed agnostic until he faced death when he was assailed by a powerful temptation to believe in a God who would judge him. He summoned a friend to reassure him that God did not exist.

We are all human beings, cut from the same cloth so to speak. We drift apart, however, and lose sight of our essential ambiguity. We are neither beings of pure faith nor beings of pure doubt. We are a mixture of each, in varying proportions. If Pope Benedict XVI and Fidel Castro can have a civil conversation with each other, there is a spark of hope for any two human beings, no matter how much they differ culturally and personally, to engage in meaningful dialogue with each other.

Section 3

The Importance of Life

The Heart Is a Lonely Hunter

The Heart Is a Lonely Hunter is the title of Carson McCullers's best-selling 1940 novel which was adapted to film in 1968 starring Alan Arkin. The story centers on the moral isolation of John Singer, a deaf mute. His heart, like that of many others is frustrated in trying to bring his heart's desires to their natural fulfillment.

We may apply this poignant notion of the heart as a lonely hunter to the human fetus whose heart, like any other heart, seeks a fulfillment which sometimes, like John Singer's, ends in tragedy. The heart symbolizes the human and is regarded as a center of benevolence. The "Heartbeat Law" in South Carolina restricts abortion after the heart begins to beat, which is around six weeks. The state's "Right to Know Act," which amended the state's laws regulating abortion at state licensed facilities, was signed into law on June 24, 2010.

Planned Parenthood lost in its attempt to weaken South Carolina's heartbeat law by allowing abortion until around the 22nd week when the heart is fully formed. Lawyers for the Palmetto State argued successfully that the baby's heart is beating six weeks into gestation even if it is not fully formed at that point.

It is most interesting to note how International Planned Parenthood has responded to fetal heartbeat laws. It strongly objected to them because they are "controversial," offer "no medical purpose and only serves to humiliate women."

In this brief critique that we have cited lies a plethora of deceptions. First, the fact that something is controversial is insufficient reason to eliminate it. Nearly every moral issue is fraught with controversy. Dismissing something because it is controversial may give the appearance of being wary, but it is a firm choice to decide an issue in favor of a certain party. A more judicious approach would be to resolve a controversial issue in the light of which side is more reasonable.

Secondly, a moral issue can be relevant even though it is not medical. With regard to the heartbeat law, its relevance is to apprise the mother more specifically of what she is doing. A true choice is based on knowledge. Without knowledge, choice is replaced by a guess, or what amounts to a stab in the dark. To enlighten a pregnant woman of what is involved in an abortion is to help her to make an informed choice. Planned Parenthood surreptitiously wants the woman to be kept in the dark. The abortion giant in this instance is not being pro-choice, but pro-abortion. It is a matter of fact that when a woman views her developing child through ultrasound, that she often changes her mind and decides to keep her child. Apparently, this is something that Planned Parenthood dreads.

Apart from the issue of choice, information that is not exactly medical is always pertinent. To overlook the personality of a patient and reduce her to a biological organism is inhuman. A doctor deals with a human being not simply a collection of organ systems. One of the sources of loneliness in the contemporary world is a lack of recognizing that a person is far more than a corporeal object. A pregnant mother has a relationship with her child in the womb. This relationship is not exactly medical, but it is surely relevant.

Perhaps the most outrageous "reason" for opposing the heartbeat law is the notion that a pregnant woman's clearer knowledge about the nature of her growing child will "humiliate" her. The fear that pertinent knowledge will cause humiliation would justify shutting down education everywhere. Knowledge enlightens; it does not humiliate. What possible justification could there be for a woman to be humiliated when she views her unborn child with the aid of a sonogram? She is not viewing Frankenstein's monster. Quite the contrary, she is viewing her child, however small, but a human being that possesses a heart. The great irony here is that the fetus does have a heart, but one has reason to wonder if the same can be said of Planned Parenthood.

The South Carolina "Right to Know Act," which amended the state's laws regulating abortion at state licensed facilities, was signed into law on June 24, 2010. The law states that abortions cannot be performed after an ultrasound can detect "cardiac activity, or the steady and repetitive rhythmic contraction of the fetal heart, within the gestational sac." Republican Gov. Henry McMaster's spokesman, Brandon Charochak, stated, after the ruling, that, "Life will continue to be protected in South Carolina, and the governor will continue his fight to protect it." The Act counters Planned Parenthood's reluctance to acknowledge that a woman has a right to know what abortion involves.

The "Heartbeat Law" and the "Right to Know Act" ensure that both a woman and the unborn child are respected insofar as she has a right to know about the child, and that child has a right to life once its heartbeat has been demonstrated. There should not be a moral isolation between the pregnant mother and her child in the womb. Planned Parenthood's defeat in attempting to extend the time for abortion is a victory for both mother and child. The more we know about the thought processes of Planned Parenthood, the more we know that it is on the side of the kind of moral isolation that characterizes the unborn child as a "lonely hunter."

Life is not a Playground

We never lose our need for play. But there are times when we must set play aside to deal with the serious side of life. Play describes the delightful world of the child. As long as it lasts, it is enjoyed as a world that is free of conflicts and anxieties. An adult may enter this world and share in the child's delight. But the adult cannot reside in this world, though he can make the occasional visit to refresh his soul. Peter Pan is ever playful, but he never grows up to enjoy the finer things of life. Remaining a Playboy is a parody of a human being. It is a refusal to grow up. Maturity is the willingness to enter the real world where conflict is unavoidable and where courage and wisdom are demanded.

The ancient Greek philosopher, Heraclitus, offered us an important insight into the paradox of human existence when he stated that unwise people "do not understand how that which differs with itself is in agreement: harmony consists of opposing tension, like that of the bow and the lyre." As a rule, people do not like tensions. They can cause severe anxieties. But the kind of tensions to which Heraclitus refers are the normal tensions in life that the mature person must accept. They are tensions that can bring about a fuller appreciation of things.

The "unwise people" like freedom, but not restraint; love, but not responsibility; choice, but not exclusion; marriage but not fidelity; and life but not death. Let us consider these oppositions one at a time.

Freedom and Restraint: Freedom is on the lips of every politician, but it is rare, indeed, that they speak of restraint. Edmund Burke understood how freedom will run amok unless it is tied to restraint. "But what is liberty," he wrote, "without wisdom, and without virtue? It is the greatest of all possible evils; for it is folly, vice, and madness, without tuition or restraint." For Daniel Webster, "Liberty exists in proportion to wholesome restraint."

Freedom (or liberty) sounds eminently positive and desirable when contrasted with restraint, which seems to put an end to freedom and spoil the fun. Yet restraint is necessary to save freedom from becoming omnivorous. "Absolute freedom leads to absolute tyranny," as Dostoevsky wisely pointed out.

Love and Responsibility: There is no end of songs and poems and tributes about love. We do not find the word "responsibility" honored in such encomia. It seems to be a rather cumbersome word. It does not stir the emotions. But if love is not wed to responsibility, it cannot be love. Responsibility is love's twin, though it lacks love's publicity. Love is deed. It cannot remain in limbo. It must act in order to promote the good of the beloved. Love responds to the needs of the other. Love cannot be standoffish. It hurries to the needs of someone who is in need. Responsibility is not a burden; it is a fulfillment. Joined to love, it ensures that love will last. In Sonnet 116, Shakespeare says that "love is not love which alters when it alteration finds . . . O no, it is an ever-fixed mark that looks upon tempests and is never shaken."

John Paul II's classic, *Love and Responsibility* accords equal value to these two words that are often separated. Love may be spontaneous, but responsibility gives love its practical reality.

Choice and Exclusion: Abortion advocates use the word "choice" as if it were an entire philosophy unto itself. Choice seems positive, personal, and unassailable. The plain fact of the matter is that every time a person makes a choice, he is excluding something that is not contained in his choice. To choose this house is the exclude all other houses. To purchase this particular automobile, is to say goodbye to all others.

"Every act of the will," wrote G. K. Chesterton, "is an act of self-limitation. To desire action is to desire limitation. In that sense every act is an act of self-sacrifice." Abraham Lincoln shares the tale of the farmer who claimed that he was not greedy. He just wanted the land that bordered his. Here is a joke and an insight woven together. Adam and Eve's cardinal sin was that they rejected any limitation.

Marriage and Fidelity: It has been said, rather facetiously, that the plural of spouse is spice. Is marriage a trap? Did Socrates die from an overdose of wedlock? To many, marriage seems terribly limited. Fidelity, remaining faithful to one's partner, however, is really an integral part of the marriage bond, where two are united in one flesh. To cite Chesterton once again, "Keeping to one woman is a small price for so much as seeing one woman." Intemperance and greed can be self-destructive.

Life and Death: We do not want to die. Yet death urges us to live while we have the opportunity. We do not have all the time in the world. We must make hay, according to the proverb, while the sun shines. Death is the boundary of life. It surrounds us and urges us to act. *Memento mori* also means *Memento vitam*. Death prevents us from sinking into lassitude. It is our alarm clock that wakens us to live.

It has been said that a wise man hears one word, but understands two. He hears freedom and understands restraint, he combines love with responsibility, he adds exclusion to choice, and fidelity to marriage. He understands that life includes death. He is one important step above the crowd that hears only what it wants to hear. But the single-word philosophy is sterile, unproductive, and barren. Life is not a playground. It is more than that. It is a workshop.

Baseball is not Life

I shall begin by enunciating the premise that the life that God has granted us is richer, more meaningful, and more important than any of the gifts we have given ourselves, such as our possessions, our artifacts, our entertainments, and our amusements. We are tempted to believe that the things we enjoy in life are more important than life itself.

My subject is the beguiling world of baseball. Has baseball, we may ask, affectionately known as America's "pastime," become larger than life? For some people, indeed, baseball is greater than life. "People ask me what I do in winter when there's no baseball," said baseball immortal, Rogers Hornsby. "I'll tell you what I do," was his response, "I stare out the window and wait for spring." The time between "the World Series and spring training," writes George Will, is a "wasteland that stretches like the Sahara."

Donnie Moore, a relief pitcher for the California Angels committed suicide because he could not forgive himself for the home run he surrendered to the Boston Red Sox in a 1986 playoff game. Ralph Branca needed lengthy psychiatric assistance to deal with giving up the famous "Shot Heard 'Round the World" to Bobby Thomson on October 3, 1951that won the pennant for the New York Giants. In the words of one reporter, Branca became part of a Shakespearean tragedy. How important is baseball? Can the misfortunes that take place on the field spoil the rest of one's life? Can our own creations, such as baseball, become more important than the life that God has given us?

Angelo Bartlett Giamatti was the 7th Commissioner of Major League Baseball. He authored a book titled, *Take Time for Paradise,* in which he sees baseball as a powerful metaphor for the time before the Fall. His thesis for his doctoral dissertation from Yale University was the role of the garden in Renaissance literature, a study which helped to form his belief that the baseball field is America's most important "garden." If Giamatti did not think that baseball is larger than life, at least, he wrote about it in mythic terms.

Baseball "is designed to break your heart," he wrote ... "The game begins in the spring, when everything else begins again, and it blossoms in the summer, filling the afternoons and evenings, and then as soon as the chill rains come, it stops and leaves you to face the fall all alone. You count on it, rely on it to buffer the passage of time, to keep the memory of sunshine and high skies alive, and then just when the days are all twilight, when you need it most, it stops."

Baseball "stops" when the last pitch is thrown in the World Series. But life goes on. We do not need baseball as a lifetime companion. The bats, gloves, and balls are stored away for the next season. The stadia become vacant. Players return to their homes where contests no longer, at least for a while, distract them from life.

Baseball is an institution that is solidly anchored to the past. Babe Ruth, Ty Cobb, Joe DiMaggio, and Ted Williams continue to be part of the game as much as they ever were. Baseball cannot forget, nor can it forgive. When Fred Snodgrass passed away in 1974 after a successful career as a businessman, his obituary read, "Fred Carlisle Snodgrass, who muffed an easy fly that helped to cost the New York Giants the 1912 World Series, died today at the age of 86." The hapless are remembered as comedy. The heroes are enshrined in a Hall of Fame. Baseball can arouse fierce passions.

"I'd walk through hell in a gasoline suit to play baseball," said Pete Rose. And it can be a most fretful experience. "A baseball game is simply a nervous breakdown divided into nine innings," wrote Earl Wilson who managed to play for 11 seasons in the Major Leagues.

Human beings have always been tempted to worship their own creations. The Golden Calf is a prime example. In Greek mythology, Pygmalion, a sculptor, produced a statue representing his ideal of womanhood. One of the lessons associated with the Pygmalion myth is that we cannot create life, no matter how skilled we may be, on our own. That is the exclusive province of God. Nonetheless, we are tempted to take our creations too seriously and as a result begin to stray from life. It is said that Michelangelo tapped one of his creations and bid it to speak. Then comes the frustration that our creative powers have limitations. Our assignment in life is to worship God and attend dutifully to our life's responsibilities.

Baseball has had a serious problem concerning players taking performance enhancing drugs. One way of looking at this phenomenon lies in the frustration that some athletes have in being only themselves and not "supermen." The comic strip Superman is a modern myth, someone no one can imitate, but someone about whom we can dream. The "field of dreams" is exactly that. But our salvation depends, not on dreams, but on how faithfully we utilize the talents that God gave us.

Major League Baseball, we must remember, despite its appeal, its grandeur and its high level of production, remains just a game. Life may not seem to match baseballs' glamor, but our task is to find in life something far richer. We are commanded, as a matter of fact, to love God and neighbor. Herein, is our true destiny and our real drama.

Football and the Pro-Life Movement

Football has its rules, and penalties are issued when they are violated. Morality has its rules, and punishment is in store for those who violate them. It should not be surprising, then, that there are staunch pro-life football players who are aware that the violation of moral rules can be damaging to society.

Benjamin Watson was a first-round selection of the New England Patriots and earned a Super Bowl ring in his rookie year. In 2018 he won the Bart Starr award as the NFL player who "best exemplifies outstanding character and leadership in the home, on the field, and in the community." He and his wife, Kristen, have founded "The Watson Seven Foundation," a non-profit organization whose mission is to strengthen families. The Watson's have 7 children of their own.

Watson is the author of *The Fight for Life: Roe, Race, and a Pro-Life Commitment to Justice* (2023). "We are in a new fight for life," he states. "We are a year past Roe being overturned and I think over this last year, so many of us who call ourselves pro-life have tried to figure out what does that mean now for a pro-life movement that wants to make abortion both unthinkable and unnecessary."

He does not believe it is enough to place legal restrictions on abortion. A higher and more complete calling must deal with the factors that propel women to have an abortion by removing the obstacles that stand in the way of choosing life. Watson's view goes beyond the abortion issue and deals with problems associated with race, poverty, and the family.

Ben Watson took issue with Kamala Harris who said, in a town hall event in Michigan with Oprah Winfrey, that Donald Trump's position on abortion was responsible for the death of Amber Nicole Thurman. Watson responded to Harris's claim by pointing out that Thurman's death was caused by "complications from legal abortion drugs and gross medical malpractice. He maintained that the woman should have been treated immediately by physicians who waited too long to intervene. Kamala was distorting the facts. "Georgia's pro-life law is not the issue," said the former football star."

Former NFL player and legendary coach, Tony Dungy, also took strong issue with Kamal Harris. The current vice-president posted on social media a claim that she had made in her debate with Donald Trump, namely that, "One does not have to abandon their faith or deeply held beliefs to agree: The government, and certainly Donald Trump, should not be telling a woman what to do with her body."

Apart from the egregious error that an unborn child is part of a woman's body, Harris employed an indefensible and highly ambiguous use of the word "faith." Dungy struck back: "Dear VP Harris: I hear you make this statement all the time. Exactly what 'faith' are you talking about when you say you don't have to abandon it to support abortion?" "Are you talking about the Christian faith that says all babies are made in the image of God (Gen 1:26), that God places them in the womb (Jer 1:5) and that we should not take any life unjustly (Luke 18:20)? Are you talking about that faith or some nebulous, general 'faith' that says we're good enough, and smart enough to make our own decisions? What 'faith' are you talking about?" Faith would, indeed, be meaningless if it embraced contradictories.

Kamala Harris is banking on the ignorance of her listeners. She is attempting to make abortion—the willful destruction of one's child in the womb—compatible with all religious faith. This is not being "liberal," but being reckless. Harris has pledged to sign a federal abortion law. In her debate with Donald Trump, she remained silent when asked if she would approve any restrictions to abortion. Surely abortion should be restricted from a woman who wants to give birth to her child. No restrictions at all would leave no room for a live birth. Kamala Harris does not understand how extreme her position is on abortion. Nor does she have any respect for the faith of Christians.

Harrison Butker, kicker for the Kansas City Chiefs, is not shy about his Catholic faith. He was not at all intimidated by those in the media who took exception to his commencement address at Benedictine College. He did not buckle under pressure. He saw no reason to apologize for his faith in "timeless Catholic values." Like Vince Lombardi of yore, he stood firm on faith, family, and football.

Vince Lombardi is arguably the greatest coach in NFL history, leading his Packers to the first two Super Bowl victories. The Lombardi trophy, appropriately named after him, is awarded to each year's Super Bowl champion. No coach ever achieved more success in shorter time than Vince Lombardi. He finished his career with a remarkable 89-29-2 record. But he was also a daily communicant Catholic, a man of strong faith. Lombardi considered it the greatest day of his life when he received his alma mater Fordham University's Insignis Medal for "Distinction in service to God through excellence in his chosen profession."

It is unimaginable, considering Lombardi's strong Catholic faith, that he would have ever countenanced abortion. Kamala Harris cannot speak for him. In fact, she has trouble speaking for herself. She is reluctant to admit the extremism of her abortion stance. But she is not hesitant to disparage the genuine faith of others. Can she continue to pull the wool over people's eyes?

St. Thomas Aquinas on the Abortion Issue

St. Thomas Aquinas never wrote explicitly on abortion. However, he bequeathed to posterity philosophical principles that allow us to deal with the issue intelligently. His thought is readily available and easily adaptable to an issue as divisive as abortion.

The first point to be made is the distinction between the intellect and the will. It is incontestable that we all possess these two faculties. The term "intellect" is associated with the word "intelligence" which, in turn, is derived from the Latin *intus leggere*, or reading into. The intellect is our faculty of knowing. It is naturally ordained to know the truth. Therefore, it reads into things, understands them as they are in their own being. The object of the will is the good. The will is naturally ordained to choose what is good, either a real good or an apparent good.

The intellect and will work together. The intellect provides the will that which it can choose. The will is unable to function without the intellect, just as the digestive system has nothing to digest in the absence of food. The will moves the intellect to act, just as the ringing of an alarm clock urges us to get out of bed.

The intellect and will are in harmony with each other as are the lungs and the heart. They flourish in tandem, wither when separated.

Aquinas speaks of the primacy of the intellect. By analogy, this simply means that we look before we act. Understanding precedes choice.

A crucial point in the thinking of Aquinas is that we should not remain indifferent to truth. In fact, we should love the truth and eagerly pass it on to the will. Philosophy is the *love* of wisdom not merely its acquisition. For the Angelic doctor, one is not truly a philosopher unless he loves the truth. Love demands that we assent to the truth we know.

The Thomistic scholar, Etienne Gilson has offered us a model of the disciple of St. Thomas as a person "of relentless will to know, coupled with an absolute intellectual respect for the truth." This type of person is admittedly rare. Accordingly, Aquinas states that "those who wish to undergo such a labor *for the mere love of knowledge* are few, even though God has inserted unto the minds of men a natural appetite for knowledge." The unadulterated search for truth, according to Aquinas is rarer in adolescence: "In youth," Aquinas writes, "when the soul is swayed by the various movements of the passions, it is not a suitable state for the knowledge of such lofty truth." These observations, however, do not depreciate the value and importance of philosophy. Truth remains truth, wisdom remains wisdom regardless of how difficult it is to attain and how infrequently it is possessed.

An additional quality that a seeker of truth must possess, for Aquinas is a tranquility of mind (*doctrina debet esse in tranquillitate*)." The philosopher must possess a certain purity of mind so he is not detracted by things that are secondary. He must also abide those who reject a truth simply because they find it disagreeable. A philosophy teacher will find many a student who is actually angered by a particular truth. An extreme example of this is attacking someone who presents an unfavorable idea in the vain hope that assaulting that person will somehow abolish the idea. Ideas are invincible

Let us now enumerate the tools that Aquinas has provided us in order to deal effectively with the abortion issue: 1) The integration of the intellect and will, together with the realization that the will cannot operate without the intellect. 2) The primacy of the intellect. 3) The demand for love in the pursuit of truth. 4) A purity and tranquility of mind that enjoys a freedom from alien distractions. 5) Respect for truth even though particular truths may be unpopular.

The primary error of abortion advocates is the denial of the role of the intellect. Pro-life advocates continue to produce a wealth of scientifically based data showing the nature of the unborn child. The abortion movement separates the intellect from the will and operates solely on pro-choice rhetoric that is limited to the will. But the will has no power of its own. It relies on the intellect to provide it with something it can choose. Without the intellect, the will is inert.

The intellect comes first. We must understand before we act. The abortion promoters, by endowing an erroneous primacy to the will, cannot begin to justify their position. In addition, by treating extrinsic factors as if they were essential, they lack a purity of mind that shields itself against such distractions. Furthermore, many who favor abortion find certain truths unpalatable and attack pro-lifers as if their assault can eradicate the ideas they hold. Finally, it does not appear that those who promote abortion are framing arguments that have been inspired by love.

It is reasonable to believe that if St. Thomas were alive today and viewed the current abortion issue, he would have denounced the rationalizations for abortion for all the reasons cited above. He would have added that the so-called reasons for abortion are loveless, juvenile, ill thought out, and indicative of mental immaturity.

We do not have Aquinas with us today, but that does not prevent us from employing his principles to create a dialogue that is placed on a reasonable foundation.

Section 4

The Path of the Christian

Where Is My Authentic Place?

In addition to the great question, "Who am I?" is the question, "Where should I stand?" I fail in my vocation if I am not in the right place. Should it be in marriage or the single state, in a seminary or convent? It is a vexing question and we can miss our "authentic place" by a single degree. In Shakespeare's *Troilus and Cressida* (Act. 1, scene 3), Ulysses strongly urges his troops to, "Stand in authentic place." He appeals to the order of the universe and what calamities would befall man if this order became disordered:

> The heavens themselves, the planets,
> and this center,
> Observe degree, priority, and place,
> Insisture, course, proportion, season, form,
> Office, and custom, in all line of order.
> But by degree stand in authentic place?
> Take but degree away, untune that string,
> And hark what discord follows. Each thing ⟨meets⟩
> In mere oppugnancy. The bounded waters

> Should lift their bosoms higher than the shores
> And make a sop of all this solid globe.

We can perform great good when we are standing in our authentic place and great harm when we are standing in the wrong place.

At a presidential campaign rally in October, 2024, Kamala Harris ridiculed two college students for proclaiming, "Christ is King." She told them, "You're in the wrong crowd." They were, as far as Harris was concerned, standing in the wrong place.

Dr. Ben Carson, world-renowned pediatric surgeon and former presidential candidate, would not allow her comment to go unanswered. He cited a passage in Matthew 12:34 which states, "Out of the abundance of the heart the mouth speaks." He then said that "She didn't have time to think about what she was going to say, so maybe she's the one who doesn't belong. Maybe we should be thinking about that."

Harris supports abortion without restrictions and supports Planned Parenthood as well as the LGBTG+ consortium. Her commitment is manifestly anti-Christian? Can Christians be in the wrong place where they are defending Christianity? Can their political views be un-American where they support the United States Constitution and what America has championed for more than 200 years?

Carson pointed out that in the last election twenty million evangelical Christians did not vote. "Think about the power that exists in the people who believe in God," Carson said. "We don't have to be victims, we don't have to complain. We can absolutely control the direction of our nation, but we have to get involved to do it." What he was inferring is that all Christians should stand in their authentic place. If they do not, there will be a large price to pay. And it will be the Christians who will bear the brunt of the cost.

Dr. Carson has a word of advice for Christians who were hesitant to choose between two bad candidates. Unless Jesus Christ is on the ballot, he states, there will always be two less than worthy candidates. Carson is a man to be admired, for standing in his authentic place" from which he has done much good. He is, as it were, a disciple of Abraham Lincoln who advised us to "Be sure to put your feet in the right place, then stand firm." We must stand firm, for the wind that assails us is not trying to knock us down, but trying to make us stronger. And from the pen of Marcus Aurelius, "Be like the cliff against which the waves continually break; but it stands firm and tames the fury of the water around it."

In addition to knowing our own authentic place, we should also be wise to those who do not. Demagogues, adulterers, thieves, embezzlers, imposters, charlatans, and frauds are not standing in their authentic place. Every place is accompanied by an opportunity for good or for bad. We ask ourselves the question, "Is this where I belong?" The answer will be "yes," if it gives us peace and allows us to perform good works.

A person may receive a licence to practice medicine, another may pass the bar to become a lawyer, yet another may earn a Ph. D. to teach philosophy. But neither of these properly appointed individuals stands in his authentic place unless he benefits others through his enduring love.

Blessings in Perspective

As the Mass comes to a close, the priest offers a blessing to all the faithful who are gathered to celebrate the Eucharist. The participants are bidden to a realization of the omnipresence of the Triune God in whose name the final blessing is invoked: "May Almighty God bless you: the Father, and the Son, and the Holy Spirit."

In his book, *This Is the Mass,* Bishop Sheen draws attention to the solemnity of the act: "In a beautiful liturgical gesture, the celebrant raises his hands on high as though he would draw down from heaven the Grace which now goes forth with us to guard and to guide us." There was a time in which this benediction was thought to be so solemn and important an act, that it was reserved for the bishop. The venerable Latin phrase, *Benedicat, Benedictus* (may the one who is blessed bless you) emphasises the importance of the moral character of the one who gives the blessing.

The final words of the celebrant, "Go, the Mass is ended," suggest that the participants go into the world with renewed zeal for their mission and with greater spiritual strength to do good and resist evil. There is a continuity between the Mass and the world. The Mass on Sunday should not be isolated from the rest of the week.

With all these thoughts in mind, I began giving nighttime blessings to each of our five children. When they were tucked in bed I would administer a blessing, lightly pressing my thumb against their foreheads: *Nos cum prole pia, benedicat Virgo Maria* (may the Virgin Mary, with her beautiful baby, bless us). The practice became a ritual and if were tardy, the children would cry out, "I didn't get my blessing!" I felt that a fatherly blessing just prior to the children slipping off to slumber land was more salutary than saying, "Sweet dreams."

When a father confers blessing on his children, he is acting in a Christ-like manner. Christ blessed children, his apostles, the sick and the lame, the loaves for the 5,000, and the Bread at the Last Supper. Petrarch, in Sonnet XLVII blesses everything associated with his meeting with Laura: "Blessed be the hour, the day, the month, the year, the Spring, the lovely scene, the moment, the spot, etc." When a person is in love everything seems blessed. God has blessed everything, but it takes love to perceive that blessed state.

A blessing that invokes God can be distinguished from a wish that excludes Him. Nonetheless, everyone has an impulse to find God. In our secular world, however, many are reluctant to travel very far to arrive at this end. They stop at the "wish." "Have a nice day" is popular, but leaves God out of the picture.

The immensely popular movie, *Star Wars,* provided a phrase that filled a gap and captured the public imagination. It was not quite "God be with you," but it was better than "Have a nice day." "May the force be with you" was cosmic and those who used it felt in conferred genuine benefits. It was a phrase so tailor-made for a secular audience that it needed to be commemorated. Hence, its annual celebration on May 4th (may the fourth be with you). It replaced, "best wishes," "good luck," and "take care."

Several U. S. presidents would conclude their speeches with the words "God Bless America." It was offered without ceremony leaving people to wonder if it were merely politically motivated. Irving Berlin's great patriotic song, *God Bless America* (notably recorded in the stentorian style of Kate Smith) was a resounding success. It earned the composer a Gold Congressional Medal conferred by the U. S. Congress. Folk singer, Woody Guthrie, however, objected to it. He felt it was too sappy, and blindly patriotic. In response, he composed, *This Land Is My Land*. The KKK did not like it because it was composed by a person of the Jewish faith.

We bless our home, our food, our children, people who are sick, newlyweds, and anyone who is in need of comfort. We are cautioned, however, that our blessings will be beneficial in proportion to our own state of blessedness. In the Sermon on the Mount, Christ blessed the poor in spirit, those who mourn, the meek, those who hunger and thirst for righteousness, the merciful, the pure of heart, the peacemakers, and those who are persecuted. In this case, the blessedness of the one who blessed was Blessedness Himself.

General Omar Bradley, who fought in World Wars I and II, lamented that, "We have many men of science; too few men of God. We have grasped the mystery of the atom and rejected the Sermon on the Mount. Man is stumbling blindly through a spiritual darkness while toying with the secrets of life and death." Bradley spoke these words on Armistice Day in 1948. But they still ring true. The current secular world has not only rejected the Sermon on the Mount, but has also rejected the entire Bible.

"It is more blessed to give than to receive," (Acts 20:35). It is also blessed to bless. As Shakespeare says of mercy, "It is twice blest; It blesseth him that gives and him that takes (*The Merchant of Venice,* Act 4: scene 1). Let us be prodigal, then, in giving blessings to our friends and neighbors.

The Freedom to be Reasonable

For most people, freedom and reason are separate faculties. They entertain the illusion that freedom can stand alone. But this is a very serious mistake. If we try to imagine pure freedom, we run into a wall. Pure freedom, if it could exist, would be paralyzing. It would get us nowhere. As soon as we would chose something, we would no longer have this elusive freedom, since we would have surrendered our freedom to the thing we chose. Isolated freedom is not real; it is only something that many people fancy in their desire to simplify things.

Why, then, do people talk about freedom as something to be cherished? Freedom is certainly to be cherished, but the freedom that people praise is usually "freedom from," which is incomplete freedom. This freedom is experienced when a person is released from authoritarianism, tyranny, or slavery. But the joy is in the thrill of being released, not in the freedom itself. After being released from prison, let's say, one says to himself, "now what."

At this point, one has the freedom to use reason in order to choose what is best for himself. This is freedom "for." The essential importance of freedom is to allow a person to use reason for his own good. But it is precisely at this juncture that a serious problem arises. How do I know what I should choose? The world has many ideas about what is good for me. Should I permit alien thought to rule my life? Or can I, through personal effort, choose my own way of life? And how can I be sure that my choice is the best choice I can make?

It is not easy, living in the midst of a hundred outside voices, to resist their allure and be an independent thinker. At the same time, I must resist the urges placed on me by my own ego.

Erich Fromm wrote *Escape from Freedom* in 1941, a work that still resonates with relevance. The central thesis of the book is that being free to be a truly authentic person and live responsibly is not only difficult, but it can also be experienced as a burden. Then comes the desire to be released from such a burden, released from freedom, and submit to one external authority or another.

According to Fromm, "Modern man lives under the illusion that he knows 'what he wants,' while he actually wants what he is supposed to want. In order to accept this it is necessary to realize that to know what one really wants is not comparatively easy, as most people think, but one of the most difficult problems any human being has to solve. It is a task we frantically try to avoid by accepting ready-made goals as though they were our own."

Therefore, it is not unusual for people to seek "escape" from freedom in order to make their lives a little easier and not so burdensome. Escaping from freedom belies the notion that our desire for freedom is unqualified. Freedom is not enough. People also need the integrity and determination to be true to themselves and maintain their freedom so their reason can function as it should in a person's best interest.

Fromm argues that "Man does not suffer so much from poverty today as he suffers from the fact that he has become a cog in a large machine, an automaton, that his life has become empty and lost its meaning." As a pundit once expressed it, playing on Descartes' famous "*Cogito ergo sum,*" "Cog ergo sum." Nothing is more important for the individual human being than to be himself. But this is an endeavor, so difficult for the mere mortal, that it invites the grace of God.

Thomas a Kempis coined the phrase, "*Da mihi scire quod sciendum est*" (God grant me the wisdom to know what I must know). We can call upon God to help us to know what we should know and avoid what we should not know. In other words, God can assist our reason so that it freely chooses what is truly good for us.

The Catholic Church has always promoted personal authenticity. The saints are proof of this. This authenticity requires the freedom to be reasonable. At the same time, being reasonable is choosing what is good. Freedom, reason, and grace, blended together, is what people truly want, not the mirage of freedom or reason dissociated from truth.

In his *Summa Theologica* (*De Veritate* 24, 2), St. Thomas Aquinas states that, "The whole root of liberty is constituted in reason" (*Totius libertatis radix est in ratione constituta*). If reason is suppressed, then freedom (or liberty) is suppressed along with it.

Once we gain freedom "from" oppression, we are faced with a difference side of freedom: freedom "for." Then reason is called upon to explain to us what this new freedom is for. And it is for our personal good. We should champion reason as much as we champion freedom, for the two are inseparable. And yet, the tandem of freedom and reason cannot succeed without its possessor being faithful, through knowledge, grace, and hard work, with what is best for him. This formula cannot be reduced to a brace of syllables, but it is the key to an authentic life.

Four Things to Consider before Making a Proper Choice

Choice is not self-justifying. If it were, any choice, not matter how reckless, impulsive, malicious or pure evil, would be justified. This amorality, performed on a national level would mean the total destruction of a country. What, then, makes a choice a proper one as opposed to the aberrant kind? Four considerations, especially for Christians, must be taken in consideration. If I am to make a proper choice, especially in matters of importance, I must ask the following questions: 1) How does this this choice affect me? 2) Am I choosing something that is good? 3) Am I being true to myself in making this particular choice? 4) How does my choice square with God?

Let us take a simple example. I find a wallet that contains $100 in cash. But it also has the address of the owner. What should I do? Should I keep the money or should I return it to the owner. Let us suppose that I keep the money. What affect does that have on me? Well, it makes me a thief! I may not like that appellation. It is not consistent with my self-image. I take comfort in knowing that I will not be prosecuted since my choice is purely private. Therefore, I am not legally a thief. Nonetheless, stealing marks me a thief, though I might protest vehemently against that label.

On the other hand, suppose I return the wallet and the money it contains to its rightful owner. What does that make me? Well, it makes me an honest man, one who is acting according to the norms of justice. It makes it easier for me to live with myself. I have made the judicious choice.

My choice to keep the money cannot be regarded as a good act, since it steals from another what rightly belongs to him. The $100 may be very important to its owner. I know nothing about his financial situation, but that is not essential. The main point is that in keeping the money I am doing something wrong. The good choice is to return it to the one who has rightful claim to it.

The truth is that the wallet and all that it contains belongs to its owner. In stealing the money, I am contradicting a truth, pretending that the money belongs to me and not to its legal owner. Whatever rationalizations I invent are false. They make me a liar to myself. If I accept these rationalizations (I really need the money) I set myself on a ruinous path. Can I be trusted? Is this act of petty larceny a prelude to further improper choices?

God made it crystal clear that stealing is wrong when He issued the Eighth Commandment, "Thou shall not steal." From His perspective, stealing, which is an act of injustice violates human community. It brings about a situation in which people cannot trust each other. Stealing is obviously incompatible with a just society.

By abiding by these four considerations, our choice reflects self-respect, respect for others, honesty, and regard for the will of God. A proper choice is blessed fourfold.

Although stealing is rampant in society, the four considerations concerning theft do not meet with scorn or strong opposition. Even people who steal do not publicly support thievery. Also, they do not vilify those who affirm the four considerations we have enumerated.

Moral issues become controversial when people deny the validity of any one of the factors that are needed in order to make a proper choice. Abortion is controversial. On the one hand, people rationalize it solely in terms of choice, eliminating all the relevant factors. A woman who chooses an abortion, which kills the unborn child, is a killer. This word my sound unduly harsh, but there is no way around it. We kill bugs, crab grass, and germs. Here, no one rebels against the word. But with regard to abortion, the term "killer" is obliterated under the weight of choice. The word "murder" is sometimes applied, but this word is more jurisprudential, being associated with court proceedings.

Secondly, abortion kills an unborn human being. This is the very act that is fully intended. But the unborn child is a good. Abortion is destructive of a good. Thirdly, in an attempt to sanitize the choice for abortion, the truth of what is transpiring must be rejected. It is difficult, as many women have found, to live with the lies associated with abortion. Therefore, they retreat into an ideology. In order to protect their thin rationalizations from being exposed, they often become hostile to people who enunciate the truth of abortion. Finally, it is incontestable that God, whose 6th Commandment forbids killing ("Thou shall not kill") would not approve the de-creation of the human beings whom He has created. To accept abortion is to abolish all four considerations that are needed in order to make a proper choice.

Prior to abortion, many people make other improper choices that lead to abortion. Nowadays, people reject the term "fornicator" because it seems either judgmental or insulting. But the validity of the term remains no matter how much it is despised. People can live from one improper choice to another.

When we make proper choices, we live rightly. When we neglect what justifies our choices, we surrender to a series of improprieties that, if not checked in time, can lead to moral ruin. This does not reflect a "conservative" approach, but one that agrees with common sense.

Jacques Maritain and the Apparition at La Salette: A Postscript

I very much enjoyed Suellen Brewster's two-part presentation on the message of La Salette that appeared in Catholic Exchange. It may be of interest to her readers to become acquainted with what the eminent Catholic philosopher, Jacques Maritain, had to say about the Apparition. The source of my postscript is Maritain's *Notebooks*.

Maritain and his wife, Raissa, had been greatly moved by the Apparition. As Jacques writes: "But before all and above all, the mystery which struck the heart and which one will never finish scrutinizing, is that of the tears shed by Her whom all generations must call blessed, the mystery of the suffering manifested by the incomparably glorious *Theotokos*, weeping before two shepherds over the hard-heartedness of men and announcing great misfortunes."

Maritain reflected on Mary's words, "you will make this known to *all my people*," and decided to apply his intelligence and artistry to write a treatise to do his part in making the message of La Salette better known to the world. At that time, in 1915, the majority of the faithful were ignorant of the Apparition. What was more disconcerting was a marked hostility toward Mélanie, the shepherdess who, with Maximin, had witnessed the Apparition.

Maritain set before himself the task of writing about La Salette in its entirety in as objective a manner as possible and serve nothing other than the truth. He recognized that the testimony of Mélanie was most important, he began to gather the observations and memories of those who had known her well. He consulted with one priest with whom Mélanie stayed twice for a few days, and another priest with whom she lived for several months and was her confessor during this time. Both priests had been her friends and held her in great veneration. But his research did not stop there. Suffice to say that he gathered enough information to write a treatise of considerable size.

Being a man of exceptional humility and a devoted Catholic, Maritain sought the opinion of Pére Garrigou-Lagrange, himself a renowned philosopher and theologian. Maritain did not want anything of his own published without the unreserved approval of the Church. Father Garrigou-Lagrange was happy with the manuscript and said to its author, "The Blessed Virgin loves you very much. You will suffer much." Then he advised him to consult with the Pope.

Pope Benedict XV received Jacques and his wife with much kindness and listened attentively to Maritain's response to La Salette. He was convinced that the apparition was authentic but wondered whether Mélanie's words should be taken literally. He cited her youthfulness and that her imagination might have been a factor in what she said. Furthermore, the Pope was concerned about avoiding a scandal, for Mary had severe things to say about certain members of the clergy. He was worried about Catholics turning away from their priests. Although at certain moments, scandal is preferable, he agreed, but it does not seem that this is the case here.

The Pope then asked Maritain if the young philosopher believed that Mélanie's words should be taken literally. At this point, Maritain experienced a dilemma: should he contradict Benedict XV or the Blessed Virgin?" "Better to displease the Pope," he wrote in his notebook. "Yes, Most Holy Father, I believe that Mélanie was a saint and that what she reported is literally true. I had many details concerning her life. She is a stigmatist. She suffered much by fidelity to her mission." "The tears," Raissa added, "correspond well to the state of the world." The pope remained silent. He appeared to be touched. Then, he said, "Here is what you must do, Go see Our Brother . . . Cardinal Billot. He is in charge of studies; it is quite a natural introduction for you."

The Cardinal received Maritain most graciously, though he was a bit taken back by the "frightfully large manuscript." He promised to read it over the next two months and send his reply through Jacques Froissart. "You have proceeded properly," the cardinal said, and then gave Maritain his blessing.

The reply was negative. Nothing objectionable was stated concerning the manuscript. But its publication was judged to be decidedly "inopportune." Authorization for publication was, thus, refused. "The only thing to do was to obey," Maritain wrote in his *Notebooks,* "as I was prepared to do from the beginning. I had done all that I could do for La Salette; to understand this piece of work had been an obligation for me of conscience." Maritain's voluminous work was never published, and he left word that it should never be published after his death. He accepted the refusal without a trace of bitterness. In fact, he felt gratitude: "I thanked Providence for having caused it to reach, by paths which I would never have been able to foresee, persons in whose hands it was doubtless most important that it be placed."

Indeed, Mary has not forgotten La Salette. The grace from the Apparition continues to cascade upon its disciples. The Missionaries of Our Lady of La Salette, founded in 1852, is a religious congregation consisting of priests and brothers. There is also a parallel religious community of sisters called "The Missionary Sisters of Our Lady of La Salette." Their combined work has spread to North and South America, Europe, Asia, Australia, and Africa. The national shrine to Our Lady of La Salette is in Attleboro, Massachusetts. There are also shrines in Enfield and New Hampshire, as well as in Portugal, Mexico, and India. "La Salette Reflections" is a monthly online magazine.

Maximin Giraud died a holy death on March 1,1875 in his native village, Corps, France. Mélanie

Calvat died as a Catholic nun on December 15, 1904, in Altamura, Italy.

Section 5

The Blessings of Common Sense

Listening to the Word of God

If I were Stephen King, I might be tempted to write a novel about a mysterious radio that transmits only the Word of God. My story would begin with a radio hobbyist who delights in collecting old radios. He is particularly interested in their value and designs, although he is also interested in the quality of sound that they transmit. He goes into an old and somewhat dilapidated antique store. His eyes fall upon a rare Philco model 38-690 and is pleased that it is offered at an extremely low price, just $10. Apparently, the proprietor knows little about the value of vintage radios. He purchases the radio and brings it home. He is disappointed, however, that he can get only one frequency. Frustrated, he goes back to the store hoping for an exchange. His frustration turns to confusion when he discovers that the store is no longer there. He questions a passer-by about the store's mysterious disappearance only to be told that there never was an antique store on that spot.

The man now wonders if he is going mad. He goes back home and tunes his radio to the one frequency that his Philco 38-690 can pick up and listens: "This is station WGOD, the only station which is worth listening to. It is the voice of God." What happens next I leave up to my imaginary Stephen King. No doubt he would play upon the word "Philco" since it refers to the Greek word, "*philia*" which refers to love.

Pope Benedict XVI stated that, "We are no longer able to hear God. There are too many different frequencies filling our ears." In fact, a phenomenon known as "jamming" occurs when more than one station sends the same frequency at the same time. When this happens, the listener is at a loss to comprehend what he is hearing. Voices are entangled. Discernment is impossible.

Here we have an image of the modern world with all its sounds and clatter filling our ears but not conveying anything worthwhile. And yet we crave more and more frequencies. We are bombarded with what amounts to noise which, by definition, excludes intelligible meaning. How do we locate that one frequency that allows us to hear the Word of God?

In 1959, Muriel Spark wrote a rather unsettling, though perceptive book entitled, *Memento Mori* (remember, you must die). The plot is based around a group of elderly people in 1950s London, most of whom are avaricious and petty-minded. The telephone repeatedly conveys the disturbing message, "Remember, you must die." Although a detective is brought in to discover who is sending the troubling message, he is unable to trace the calls to their source. Is it God, or one of his representatives who is making the phone calls? The point of the novel is that we are easily distracted by the noise in our lives from hearing what is important. Rather, we fill our minds with trivia. It may take something of an extraordinary nature to shake us out of our lethargy.

The Word of God is something we tend to block out or even flee from. Francis Thompson, in his celebrated poem, *The Hound of Heaven,* dramatically describes man fleeing from God: "I fled Him, down the nights and down the days; I fled Him, down the arches of the years; I fled Him, down the labyrinthine ways of my own mind."

In Chapter XII of his *Confessions*, St. Augustine tells us that he heard a voice commanding him repeatedly to "take up and read." "So checking the torrent of my tears," he wrote, "I arose; interpreting it to be no other than a command from God to open the book, and read the first chapter I should find." What he read changed his life and opened the way to his sainthood: "Not in rioting and drunkenness, not in chambering and wantonness, not in strife and envying; but put ye on the Lord Jesus Christ, and make not provision for the flesh, in concupiscence. No further would I read; nor needed I."

The first requirement in listening to the Word of God is to root out any anxieties we have about what God might say. A person may be reluctant to see a doctor fearing his diagnosis. But God is love and we should be open to His message. We should trust God. The next requirement is to be silent. In this way, we shut out all the noise that could be a barrier to God's voice. What we hear may already appear in the Gospel. But, then, again, it might be personal, giving us direction in our life's journey. Secondly, we must be humble. In humility, we clear out selfish concerns and open ourselves to the one frequency that unites us to God. James tells us that, "in humility [we] receive the Word implanted, which is able to save your souls (James 1:21)." If we are too proud to let God instruct and command us, we will not profit from the Word. The next step is the willingness to put the Word into practice. This includes sharing it with others.

In finding the right frequency that connects us with God we should not expect the radio or the telephone to do the work for us. The imaginary Stephen King and Muriel Spark's novel belong to the world of fiction. We must take the initiative ourselves. Trust, silence, and humility tune us in to God's frequency and dispose us to share His message with others. And God is always at the microphone.

Heaven is not of This World

The mere fact that we are mortal is sufficient reason to exclude heaven from this world for heaven must be eternal. Yet the superstition persists that we can have heaven on earth. At best, we have glimpses or intimations of a perfect world, but they are just that. The purpose of this world is to provide a stepping stone to heaven. This world is where we purchase out ticket to paradise.

Politicians, however, think otherwise. Their political slogans indicate that we can achieve heaven on earth simply by voting for the right candidate. Despite the fact that no politician has ever materialized on his promises, this has not dampened the enthusiasm for making more completely unrealizable promises.

In 1961, John F. Kennedy had a most agreeable and inspiring slogan: "Ask not what your country can do for you--ask what you can do for your country." A more pertinent question would be, "What can I do for my family?" It is not quite clear what I can do directly for my country. In 1968, Robert Kennedy's presidential nomination campaign also had a captivating slogan: "Some people look at what is and say, why. I dream of things that have never been and say why not." People liked the optimism this slogan represented, but no one had any idea of what the dream contained. Nor could they imagine anything that never was. Martin Luther King, Jr. also had a dream, but one that had not yet begun to materialize.

The dominant slogan in 2024 for the Democratic Party, as enunciated repeatedly by Kamala Harris is: "I can imagine what can be when we are unburdened by what has been." This presumed jettison of the past, however, leaves nothing for the imagination. The past is not a burden, but something to build upon.

These slogans, typical of political rhetoric, intimate a future of unprecedented excellence, a kind of heaven on earth. But it does not take very long for such promises to become unworkable. And so, the populace needs a new candidate, one who will make the impossible realizable. This, the superstition continues unabated.

Heaven must be earned, not by casting a vote, but through love. Consider the 12 following sayings of

Christ: "Whoever has ears should hear." "Love your brother like your life." "If you do not abstain from the world, you will not find the kingdom." "The evil of the day is sufficient thereof." "Love one another as I have loved you." "It is impossible for a servant to serve two masters." "Blessed are those who have been persecuted in their heart." "Man does not live by bread alone." "Give Caesar the things that are Caesar's. Give God the things that are God's." "What comes out of your mouth will defile you." "Love your enemies and pray for those who persecute you so that you may be sons of your Father who is in heaven." "The truth will set you free."

These saying are directed to individual persons and are intended to awaken them to a better life. They convey a sense of practical realism. They also imply the great worth of the individual person. Political sayings, on the other hand, are directed to the masses and are bereft of any moral implications. The elected will do all the work, and the populace will be happy recipients.

In Colossians 3:2, St. Paul advises us to "Think about the things of heaven, not the things of earth."

In speaking of the "things of earth," he is not referring to our daily needs, but specifically to "immorality, uncleanness, lust, evil desire and covetousness." The earth has a gravitational effect on people and can drag them down. Since we are made for heaven, we should always keep in mind our ultimate destiny.

Heaven is not a myth, but something we sense from time to time. William Wordsworth, in his ode, "Intimations of Immortality from Recollections from Early Childhood," finds that "Heaven lies about us in our infancy." We sense, when we are young and innocence that everything around us is "Apparell'd in celestial light." We lose that sense as we age, though it does not completely disappear. For the poet Williams Blake attests that he could see "heaven in a wild flower." Beauty reminds us that there must be a realm in which prefect beauty resides. Love also gives us a sense of the eternal and the supremely lovable. A happy family, it has been said, is an earlier heaven.

Politicians talk about a virtual heaven on earth. Christianity insists that when we think too much about heaven on earth, we lose heaven. Or, as C. S. Lewis states, "Aim at heaven and you will get earth thrown in. Aim at earth and you get neither." For

Robert Browning, "man's reach must exceed his grasp, Or what's a heaven for." Heaven is not attainable in this world, but it draws us to it. It is, as another poet, George Herbert says, a "pulley."

Everyone wants to get to heaven, but few are willing to die. This is the great paradox of life. What we want most requires a path we desire least. Nonetheless, the more we are in touch with heaven, especially through love and beauty, the more our fear of death is softened. Heaven is not of this world, but its signature is printed everywhere, but especially in our hearts.

Is Catholicism a Religion-in-Progress?

"Hello, this is your Captain. To update you, we are travelling at 25,000 feet and moving at 500 mile per hour. We do not expect any turbulence. However, we are lost!

Or, in the words of G. K. Chesterton, "As enunciated today, progress is a comparative of which we have not settled the superlative." Long before he became president and speaking for General Electric, Ronald Reagan reminded his audience that, "At General electric, you know, 'Progress is our most important product.'"

Progress is slippery. Nonetheless, it has become the unofficial motto of the modern world. Progress is seemingly everywhere: in the automobile industry, in medicine, in communications, in travel, in food production, and in the exploration of space. Inevitably, the question arises, should the Catholic Church also be progressive?

Not being progressive invites unattractive labels: static, stagnant, rigid, conservative, and not being up to date. In the 1970's there was much talk about a Catholic/Marxist synthesis. It was said that the

Church has the love and Marxism has the structure. Further investigation, however, revealed that Marxism did not have the "structure' and the Catholicism and Marxism were entirely disjunctive belief systems.

Pope Paul VI's *Humanae vitae* disappointed many Catholics who thought that accepting contraception would be a liberal idea and bring the Church more fully into the modern world. Some Catholics left the Church over the contraception issue believing that She had become "out-dated." The rejection of the ordination of women was also seen refusing to be "progressive."

Vatican II stated that abortion is an "abominable crime." Nancy Pelosi, a self-described Catholic, inverted the phrase and insisted that withholding access to abortion is an "abominable crime." Viewing the Church as anything but progressive, Ginete Paris wrote *The Sacrament of Abortion,* making the case that the decision to abort may spring from a religious feeling that it is the right thing to do. Should the Church appease feminists by instituting abortion as Her eighth sacrament? But the Church stubbornly holds the number of sacraments to seven. Approving abortion would be regressive and rapidly drive the Church into self-destruction.

It is a great blessing that the Church has from its inception an un-barterable integrity that refuses to kowtow to the world. The Church, throughout the ages, has been a sufficient guide in leading souls to heaven. Meanwhile, the world has not been exactly a paragon of virtue. The Church has always been wise to reject the devil.

The Church is not progressive because She already has everything She needs. Being progressive is a responsibility that falls upon Her members. Rather than advance in holiness, which requires a number of difficulties and inconveniences, it is often more attractive for a person to demand that the Church undergoes change rather than the self. Naturally, if the Church made all the concessions that the "liberals" demanded, there would be no more Church. She would coincide perfectly with the secular world and render Herself entirely irrelevant. The arch-liberal says, "I can't wait until the Church catches up to me."

In his book, *Principles of Catholic Theology, Building Stones for a Fundamental Theology*, Joseph

Cardinal Ratzinger (later Pope Benedict XVI) criticizes, "That all-too-guileless progressivism . . . which happily proclaimed its solidarity with everything modern, with everything that promised progress, and strove with the self-conscious zeal of a model schoolboy to prove the compatibility of what is Christian with all that is modern . . . " The irony here is so many Christians professed a stronger religious fervor for modernism than they did for Christianity. It was as if such people were saying, "If the Church won't come to me, I will not go to the Church." Ratzinger had in mind something more fundamental, something that serves as a building block. The Church is built on a "rock," not a trend. And that is why the Catholic Church has lasted for more than 2,000 years.

Charles Péguy wrote wisely when he penned the following: "Christianity is in no way and by no means a religion-in-progress: nor (perhaps even less, so if that is possible) is it a religion of progress. It is the religion of salvation." If the word "progress" has any significance here, it is in the sense of the word used by John Bunyan in his classic, *Pilgrim's Progress* (1678). For the author, the bedrock is the Bible which inspires the pilgrim to a life of virtue. Progress, therefore, is through virtue anchored to a source that does not to be changed with the times. For a period in history Bunyan's allegory was the second most read book after the Bible.

"In a world of fugitives," wrote T. S. Eliot, "the person taking the opposite direction will appear to run away." So much attention has been devoted to the dissidents fleeing from the Church that the faithful appear to be, to cite a popular aphorism, on the wrong side of history. The problem concerning progress in the wrong direction has a long history. Pope Pius X alluded to it in a 1914 rather strong address: "Oh! How many navigators, how many pilots, and—God forbid!—how many captains, trusting in profane novelties and in the deceitful science of the age, have been shipwrecked instead of reaching port!"

The Church will continue to survive because Christ instituted Her to last. The attacks, turmoil, doubts, and deceptions serve only to prove that She is more powerful than Her adversaries. If the church is not progressive, it is because She is indestructible.

Mother Angelica vs. Charles Darwin

I was relaxing in the sun, enjoying the warmth that Old Sol generously provides. I say "relaxing" in the sense that I am not doing anything in particular. My mind, however, seldom, if ever relaxes. I spotted a tiny ant scurrying across the concrete pavement. It seemed to know where it was going and what it would do when it got there. I admired its energy. Such a tiny thing and yet it has purpose and the desire to go on living. It pleased me to witness one of God's creatures going about its work which, to it, is the most important thing in the world. God bless this tiny creature for doing exactly what its Creator wills it to do.

Ants first appeared on earth between 140 and 160 million years ago during the Jurassic Period when dinosaurs roamed the land. That would have given them enough time, according to evolutionist Charles Darwin, to change into a higher species. What that higher species might be is difficult to imagine. And yet, after this considerable amount of time, ants are still ants. Do they need a few more million years to evolve beyond their anthood? We will never know for sure. But my guess is that they will still be ants.

What the specialists (they are called myrmecologists) do know is that their extinction would prove catastrophic, for they are essential for soil aeration, fertilization, and ecological balance. If they could listen to us, we should say to them, "Please stay as you are, do not evolve, your work is very important to us." But they do this anyway and have been doing it without complaining for untold millions of years.

Anteaters have been around for about 25 million years, and they, too, are still anteaters. But they have done very little to reduce the world's population of ants. Ants and anteaters are, so to speak, "conservative," and have done a good job in avoiding progress. God anticipated the anteaters need for ants millions of years before they came into being. That is called being Provident.

According to Darwin, evolution is possible because a living organism changes, one step at a time, due to a variety of extrinsic factors. Let us go along with the great evolutionist and imagine a monkey slowly undergoing small changes until it is finally transformed into a human being. Let us say, then, that this new species, the product of untold years of evolution, is a male. Presumably, it would take as much time for a female to arrive. By that time, however, the male would have long since vanished from the planet. It would be unlikely, according to Darwinian principles, for the newly evolved being to be a male since it is only too clear that the male is ordered in a complementary fashion to the female who, at the time, did not exist. Darwin does not explain why an evolved being requires another being, one that is wholly independent, for its completion. He does not explain how two separate beings could evolve that are profoundly related to each other. If he had a sense of humor, he could have said, "It's just like a woman to be late."

Darwin, who knew absolutely nothing about micro-biology, taught that beings evolve one step at a time. There are some biological facts, however, that never entered his mind. A 10-year-old boy is composed of 28 trillion cells. To make things even more mind boggling, each cell contains 46 chromosomes arranged in pairs of two. Then, his body must integrate another 8 trillion cells for him to become a full-fledged adult male. The immune system contains 100 billion immunological receptors. And so on. None of this can be explained by a one step at a time process.

We may go a little further, concerning the prodigious and prolific nature of the human being. In order to stay healthy, 10 billion white cells and 400 billion platelets need to be produced in an individual on a daily basis. Scientists know a lot more about biology than Darwin did in 1859 when he wrote, *On the Origin of the Species.* The plain fact is that he failed to discover the origin of any species. Furthermore, the full title of his masterpiece proved that he is just as ignorant about social justice as he was ignorant about biology. The full title of his famous work is, *On the Origin of the Species, or the Preservation of Favored Races in the Struggle for Life.*

I do not think that Mother Angelica spent much time studying Darwinian evolution. She had heard, as most of us have, the notion that monkeys evolved into humans. "Why, then," she said, are there still monkeys? She also could have said, "Why are there still ants and anteaters"? The question would have annoyed Darwin. He would have countered by stating that evolution takes place in a single organism and not every individual in the entire species at the same time. OK, but the holy nun has a point. If a single monkey evolved into a single human, how then could that human procreate?

Mother Angelica's acceptance of *Genesis* puts her far ahead of Darwin's theory of evolution. Darwin tried hard to exclude the Creator and explain life in terms of chance. Yet chance cannot begin to explain the magnificent order that is found everywhere in the universe. Try as he may, the evolutionist cannot do away with God. We leave the final words to that paragon of common sense, G. K. Chesterton: "It is absurd for the Evolutionist to complain that it is unthinkable for an admittedly unthinkable God to make everything out of nothing, and then pretend that it is more thinkable that nothing should turn into everything."

America Needs Help from Above

There is a passage in *King Lear* that typifies the current turmoil in the United States: "If that the heavens do not their visible spirits send quickly down to tame these vile offenses it will come: Humanity must prey upon itself like monsters of the deep" (Act 4, scene 2, 52-55). America needs help from above.

Mindful of the seriousness of the situation, Fr. Chad Ripperger, a theologian, philosopher, and exorcist in the Denver archdiocese, has composed a prayer to Mary Immaculate, Patroness of the United States of America which he urges people to recite: The prayer, which is rather lengthy, includes the following sentence: "We consecrate to Thee the integrity of the upcoming election and its outcome, so that what is spiritually and morally best for the citizens of our country may be accomplished, and that all of those who are elected would govern according to the spiritual and moral principles which will bring our nation into conformity with the teachings of Thy Son."

The image of monsters of the deep preying upon each other is apt, for Americans are presently without a unifying principle and are consequently at war with each other. If we can spotlight one important reason, from a philosophical point of view, that helps to explain the current discord, it is an erroneous notion of freedom. America is the "Land of the free and the home of the brave." Most unfortunately, she has a confused understanding of the former, and a misguided notion of the latter.

As a jumping off point, let us refer to a remark that US Transportation Secretary, Peter Buttigieg, made during a July 29, 2024 fundraising event. He opined that abortion makes men, "More Free." This is the kind of frivolous use of the term "free" that has been exemplified more than a million times. Inevitably, it invokes the response from women, "What about our freedom." The clash between men and women over abortion is irresolvable using this simplistic notion of freedom. It is a use of freedom that invites contradictions and discord. No human society could be established on the basis of such an enfeebled understanding of freedom.

We are speaking here of freedom of choice which is our birthright. This is something we inherit. We do not achieve it. But it is a faculty that we may use virtuously or viciously. It is incapable in itself of orienting us to what is good. In this sense, it is morally neutral. To regard it as its own end is an error as great as denying its existence altogether. Freedom of choice, then, is not self-justifying. It is not an end in itself.

"A prime error," writes Jacques Maritain in his study on freedom, *Freedom in the Modern World*, "which seems to be the root error of many of our contemporaries lies in the confusion of the two kinds of freedom that we have distinguished: freedom of choice, and freedom of autonomy." The term "autonomy" may be slightly misleading, but Maritain is using it in the sense of freedom of fulfillment.

Life is not so simple that we can find our personal fulfillment simply by exercising our freedom of choice. The misdirection of this freedom can be ruinous to both self and others. The choice to abuse liquor, for example, has severely negative effects on both the self as well as on others. This is not the kind of freedom that is worthy of the human being. There must be a higher freedom, one that is the continuation and justification of one's freedom of choice. If I want to become a doctor, I have a goal to which all my free choices are subordinate. I attend medical school, study hard, develop skills, and become sensitive to the needs of patients, and so on. If all my choices line up properly, then I can enjoy the higher freedom of *being* a doctor. My choices are a means to an end. Freedom of choice is the means; freedom of fulfillment is the end. There is no point in making choices willy-nilly that invite chaos. Freedom of choice must subserve freedom of fulfillment, or it is useless.

In a broader sense, I have a destiny appointed by God. In order to achieve that destiny, I must order my choices so that each one advances me toward that appointed goal. My freedom of fulfillment, my freedom of becoming truly myself is higher and more meaningful that my ability to choose one thing at a given time.

Abortion gives men more freedom! This is, philosophically, equivalent to saying that rejecting the 10 commandments gives people more freedom. But, we must ask, freedom to do what? To dance around the golden calf? Freedom to use one's freedom of choice in a haphazard way so as never to become truly one's self? It should also be pointed out that freedom of fulfillment does not clash or contradict the freedom of anyone else. In fact, it aids and abets the freedom of others. We are best suited to help others if we are truly our God-appointed selves. Achieving freedom of fulfillment helps others on the road of their own freedom of fulfillment.

By not ordering one's freedom of choice to freedom of fulfillment, writes Maritain, man "achieves only dispersion and disintegration. The heart becomes atrophied and the senses exacerbated, or else all that is human in man recoils into a vacuum veiled in frivolity." These are strong words and help to explain the seriousness of the current situation in America. Let us all work together to achieve freedom of fulfillment.

Section 6

God is in Control

Yes, God Was Right, There Are Two Different Sexes

It has been only recently, from a historical point of view, that the distinctiveness of the two sexes has come into question. It had been universally accepted that the difference between male and female was rooted in their natures. This was the case throughout all the cultures of the world and was evident throughout the animal kingdom.

In *Genesis*, God proclaimed that there are two sexes, male and female, and that they are related to each other in a complementary fashion. This seemed to be an unshakeable matter of common sense. The new theory is that male and female are not so much natural as formed by one's environment. Was God wrong? And was common sense an unreliable tool in coming to terms with the notion as of male and female? Pope John Paul responded to the issue by putting together his "Theology of the Body" in which he affirmed what was said in *Genesis*.

The idea that environment rather than nature is the determining factor in producing male and female, man and woman, put forward largely by the university community, became the politically correct view. It became difficult to publish anything that defended both *Genesis* and common sense. A spectacular example of this is the fact that Professor Steven Goldberg's scholarly book explaining that the differences between the sexes is essentially biological was rejected 69 times by 55 different publishers before it was published to acclaim. The sheer number of rejections earned *The Inevitability of Patriarchy* a place in the *Guinness Book of Records*. The author is a man of enviable determination.

Goldberg, an honored member of the City University of New York and chairman of the sociology department, after exhaustive research, made the following observation: "I believe the evidence indicates that women follow their own physiological imperatives and that they would not choose to compete for the goals that men devote their live to attaining. Women have better things to do. Men are aware of this and that is why in this and every other society they look to women for gentleness, kindness, and love, for refuge from a world of pain and force, for safety from their own excesses. In every society a basic male motivation is the feeling that the women and children must be protected." These thoughts are congruent with research, Scripture and common sense.

Genesis tells us that Eve, a prototype of all women, was a "helper" for Adam. Acclaimed scholar, Samuel Terrien points out, in his book, *Till the Heart Sings*, that "helper" does not in any way imply subordination or involvement in menial tasks. The Hebrew word is derived from a Semitic verb (*'ezer*) which means "to deliver from death, to save from extremity." The word *'ezer* is never used elsewhere in Scripture to designate an inferior status. In fact, it is used in referring to God as the Savior of Israel. Moreover, when *Genesis* speaks of the *"two-in-one flesh,"* unity of man and woman it is stating something strikingly counter-cultural since, at that time, the woman was assimilated into the man's family. *Genesis* was not culturally determined.

Nature precedes cultural influence. Whatever culture affects, it affects something that is natural. There must be a substratum on which culture or the environment operates. Nature comes first. A woman in Pennsylvania declares for common sense when she says, "They keep telling us that men and women are the way they are because of what they've been taught, but you can go a hundred miles in any direction and not find a single person who really believes that."

No one denies that the cultural environment has an effect on men and women. A good example of how it does influence people is the fact that certain individuals are conditioned to think that the environment has a greater impact on the sexes than nature. But the environment works on people from the outside. It cannot get inside them and alter their DNA or change their hormones. Saint John Paul II, Steven Goldberg and the like, refused to be anything like products of their environment and insisted on being themselves. The environmentalists have little credibility because they maintain that they themselves have been conditioned by their environment. In this regard, they make a giant step away from objective reality as well as from their own personal identities. The Socratic dictum prevails: "Know thyself."

The loss of common sense is to be found mostly among intellectuals who want to say something that has never been said before. Vanity and ambition can be effective enemies of common sense.

The primacy of nature is exhibited in small children. As observation informs us, boys tend to be boys and girls tend to be girls. Also, it is only too evident that young children recognize the difference between mommy and daddy and act accordingly. In this case, little tykes can display more common sense than can be found among certain university professors.

When men are left by themselves, they tend to be coarse and aggressive. What they display is a need for the humanizing effect that women bring. It is most unfortunate that the more women imitate men and abandon their natural role as women, the more they are at the mercy of male aggression. The evidence indicates that God was right when he proclaimed that there are two sexes, male and female, and they can unite in marriage to form a two-in-one flesh unity.

What is the Mother of All Virtues?

What is the virtue that comes first, the one that is needed before any other virtue can finds its proper place? There is quite a range of opinion on this matter. The question seems to be an important one, especially for those who want to be thoroughly virtuous. Where does one start? We know when a lot of things start: the New Year on January 1, the day at daybreak, the first pangs of love, who is up first in a baseball game, and so on. *Genesis* informs us that "In the beginning God created heaven and earth." It seems that to start from the beginning is a good place from which to start.

There is a wide range of disagreement on this topic. The finest minds have given it careful attention and have offered their various opinions. For St. Augustine it is, and most emphatically, *humility*. We must empty ourselves of any taint of pride, for that vice places the willful self above the attainment of any virtue. G. K. Chesterton has stated the matter most eloquently as well as forcefully: "Pride is the falsification of fact by the introduction of self, the enduring blunder of mankind."

For St. Thomas Aquinas, the preliminary virtue must be love, for, as he argues, love is the form of all virtues. Each virtues derives its virtuousness from its root in love. Without love, there can be no virtues at all. A person may behave in a just manner, but he lacks the virtue of justice if his actions do not spring from love. One may appear to be loyal, but his inspiration may not but rooted love, but in fear of reprisals. Love differentiates the true virtues from all the counterfeits.

St. Francis of Assisi held *courtesy* in high regard. We may think of courtesy as a virtue that opens the door to other virtues. This makes sense on a practical level. A simple act of courtesy, carrying a heavy bag for an elderly lady, offering directions to a stranger, catching someone's hat that is blowing in the wind, and so on, can precipitate a friendship. In turn, that friendship can open the door to the development of other virtues. Courtesy is an entrance virtue that can easily be expressed between strangers.

For Dietrich and Alice von Hildebrand, the mother of all virtues is *reverence*. Dietrich was born in the city of Florence, Italy which, from an artistic point of view, is perhaps the most beautiful city in the world. Beauty inspires reverence, the appropriate respect for all things that are beautiful. Reverence causes the ego to stop in awe so that the beauty of something can be recognized and enjoyed. This attention to beauty is the first step in the formation of a beautiful character which is, simply, a person of many virtues.

The philosopher/theologian Paul Tillich. Finds *courage* to be the first virtue to be acquired and the one that sets in motion all the other virtues. He develops his thought on this point in his celebrated book, *The Courage To Be*. Tillich is looking at courage as an existentialist. Man exists in a world that is surrounded by non-being: disease, death, guilt, error, and various other factors that cause fear. It is because of this existential atmosphere where so many things can go wrong, that Tillich maintains that courage is at the very beginning of a development as authentic human beings.

One of Paul Tillich's disciples, Rollo May, a distinguished psychotherapist, pays tribute to his master in his own work, *The Courage To Create*. Winston Churchill is in agreement with Tillich and May when he declares that "Courage is rightly esteemed as the first of human qualities . . . because it is the quality which guarantees all others." Aristotle also held that courage is the primary virtue since it makes all other virtues possible.

Philosopher John Rawls, in his book, *A Theory of Justice* (1971), argues that *justice* is the first virtue of social institutions. Society is well-ordered when it is effectively regulated by a public conception of justice. Crime interferes with the public good and must be abolished. Justice, therefore, ensures the safety of the citizens of a community. Justice, in this sense, may or may not be inspired by love. But it is primary in a social sense and necessary for the good of society.

On a supernatural level, the Catholic Church teaches that there are three theological virtues, namely, faith, hope, and charity, and that the greatest of these is charity. The Church also teaches that there are four Cardinal Virtues: Justice, Fortitude, Temperance, and Prudence. Prudence is also called Wisdom, and in this since is the highest of the virtues. The word "cardinal" is derived from the Italian word, *cardine,* meaning "hinge." The cardinal virtues, therefore, are like hinges that serve to open the door to other virtues.

Humility, love, courtesy, reverence, courage, and justice, along with the theological and cardinal virtues assist a person in his moral development. They give him strength and direction. Without virtues, people are lost. Which virtue comes first may be more of an academic question than a practical one. The important thing to note is that all the virtues are linked together. No virtue exists in isolation. All virtues are desirable. Nevertheless, we hold a special place for those virtues that will naturally lead to other virtues.

Why Is Humility so Difficult to Achieve?

Humility, on the one hand, should be the easiest of all the virtues to achieve. After all, we did not create ourselves and we owe a debt of gratitude that we can never pay to our parents and all those who have contributed to our life. We are microscopic specks inhabiting a vast universe for a very brief period. As the Russian existentialist, Nikolai Berdyaev writes, "humility is ontological." By that he means that if we take an honest look at our being it tells us that we should be humble.

On the other hand, as a matter of fact, humility is the most difficult of all the virtues to acquire. Why is there such disparity between realism and fantasy? We are mortal, finite, defectible, and prone to extreme foolishness. That is nothing to be proud of. Yet pride takes hold of us and expresses itself in the three ugly daughters of ambition, boastfulness, and ostentation. We look at our existence through rose colored glasses. We are truly odd creatures.

The distinguished writer, Somerset Maugham expressed this conundrum in his biography, *The Summing Up*: "To myself I am the most important person in the world; though I do not forget that, not even taking into consideration so grand a concept as the Absolute, but from the standpoint of common sense, I am of no consequence whatever. It would have made small difference to the universe if I had never existed."

For the man who was, in his time, the world's highest paid novelist, his philosophy of life oscillated unhappily between egoism and despair. Maugham was an atheist and could not reconciles the antinomies between these two perspectives of the self and common sense. Nevertheless, he has spoken for millions who have gone through similarly unproductive struggles.

Each one of us looks out at the world from a point of consciousness. We have *our* consciousness, something that no one else has. What happens to us is supremely important. What happens to others takes place outside of our frame of reference. "I think therefore I am," said Descartes, but does his kind of thinking ratify the existence of anyone else? Given our unique way of viewing the world, it is inevitable that we assign more importance to ourselves than is reasonable. I am a subject who is the only subject for me, therefore, what happens to me is of paramount importance. I think and act as though I am the center of the universe. No wonder I have difficulty coming to terms with objectivity, truth, and common-sense realism.

But if God exists, then He, not I, occupies that center. I am important because my destiny is to serve God. In this regard, my existence and my destiny harmonize. Without God, I try vainly to reconcile contradictories.

Humility may be rare, but it does exist. I provide four examples featuring a politician, an essayist, an artist, and a novelist. Their examples inspire both admiration and imitation.

Abraham Lincoln stated in his Gettysburg Address that, "The world will little note, nor long remember, what we say here . . ." His address stands as arguably the greatest speech every given by an American politician. Many a high school student has been obliged to memorize the address. His words are not only remembered, but praised, honored, and celebrated. When we are humble, that is when we are at our best.

G. K. Chesterton, despite his astonishing talents as an artist, novelist, poet, and literary critic, like Lincoln, did not think his words would be long remembered. "I believe the biographers . . . of the future, if they find any trace of me at all, will say, Chesterton, Gilbert Keith." Those who knew him attested to his humility.

William Kurelek (1927-77) was, during his lifetime, Canada's most popular painter. A man of extraordinary humility, be believed that his paintings were meant to serve God and not for self-remuneration. His initial decision not to sign his paintings was overridden by his agent who explained that buyers wanted a signature to indicate the painting's authenticity. Kurelek obliged and signed his painting with his initials, WK, with the middle tine of the "W" rising to form a Cross. I had the pleasure of befriending William Kurelek and can attest to his genuine humility. He provided 7 sketches for my first book without charge and sent most of the proceeds from his paintings to feed the hungry.

Edward Doherty (1890-1975) was a novelist and newspaper reporter. While writing for the *Chicago Tribune,* he was reputed to have been the highest paid journalist in America. He authored "*Wisdom's Fool: a Biography of St Louis De Montfort.* Widowed twice, he married a third time, to Catherine de Hueck, founder of the Madonna House Apostolate. While married, he became a priest in the Melkite Greek Catholic Church. His grave marker in Combermere, Ontario is a summation of his life's work: "All my words for the Word." In humility we find both ourselves and our purpose in life.

C. S. Lewis has told us that "Humility is not thinking less of yourself but thinking of yourself less." Humility is not self-abnegation but accepting our empowerment from God. There can be no humility without God. Dedication to God saves us from egoism and despair. He affirms us in our being and offers us our destiny. It is only in God that we can harmonize our significance as a unique human being with our divinely appointed destiny.

In Praise of Domesticity

The telephone rang at the Hayden household, deep in suburbia. It was a special consultant to the President for cultural affairs inviting Phyllis McGinley Hayden to the White House Festival of Arts. Two thoughts crossed her mind, neither being the honor of being invited to the White House. She had to juggle her schedule to fit in an honorary degree at St. John's University in Jamaica, New York. Her second thought was "Oh, I don't like this! I like to live quietly and peacefully."

Phyllis could not hide from her fame. *Times Three*, a collection of her poems sold 80,000 copies in hard cover alone. In 1964 the University of Notre Dame conferred upon her the Laetare Medal, awarded annually to an outstanding American Roman Catholic. In making the presentation the Rev. Theodore M. Hesburgh, president of the university described her as "the most highly respected contemporary writer of light verse." Three years early, she won the Pulitzer Prize for her poetic efforts. Among her many honors are the Catholic Book Club's Campion award (1967) and the Catholic Institute of the

Press Award (1960). She was elected to the National Academy of Arts and Letters in 1955.

At the White House Festival, she was asked to recite on of her own poems. She chose *Diversity*, praising God for the variousness of his creation which includes the following stanza:

> Praise what conforms and what is odd,
> Remembering, if the weather worsens
> Along the way, that even God
> Is said to be three separate Persons.
> Then upright or upon the knee,
> Praise Him that by His Courtesy,
> For all our prejudice and pains,
> Diverse His Creature still remains.

Phyllis McGinley was born to be a poet. As far back as she could remember, her muse was coaxing her to spin thoughts in words. At the tender age of six she produced a quatrain that showed promise, if not prowess: "Sometimes in the evening/When the sky is blue and pink,/ I love to lie on the hammock/and think and think and think." "From then on", she remarked, "it never occurred to me that I wasn't going to be a poet."

Fearing that she could not make a living writing poetry, she took a job teaching English at a junior high school in New Rochelle, NY. Her principal was not enamored with her poetic extra-curricula activities, and conveyed to her his concern that they might interfere with her classroom commitments. She responded appropriately. She quit. In retrospect, it was the right thing to do.

She responded to domesticity as if it were poetry. The first of her two daughters was born in 1939. "I have never felt so divine in my life as the time before she was born. I was so full of euphoria, I was practically immune from all human illnesses." Her second daughter arrived two years later.

Phyllis McGinley was achieving something she was not supposed to achieve in the eyes of secular feminists. She was happy at home with her husband and daughters. Betty Friedan had written *The Feminine Mystique* in which she characterized the household state as nothing less than "dangerous." "It is not an exaggeration," she wrote, "to call the stagnating state of millions of American house wives a sickness."

Adding to the negative appraisal of domesticity was Simone de Beauvoir, who, in *The Second Sex,* said that submitting to housework betrays "a kind of madness bordering on perversion."

Undeterred, housewife McGinley penned *Six Pence in Her Shoe* which remained on the best-seller list for 26 weeks. Total sales soon exceeded 100,000. "I feel sorry for this younger generation," she wrote. "They've been told that they're not contributing to the world if they relax into their normal ocean of domesticity." In one of her poems, she captured the dissatisfaction of secular feminism: "Snugly upon the equal heights/Enthroned at last where she belongs,/ She takes no pleasure in her Rights/ who so enjoyed her "Wrongs."

If her poetry was critical, it was always laced with humor. And she did not fear where angels fear to tread. "For the female of the species may be deadlier than the male/but she can make a cup of coffee without reducing the entire kitchen to a shambles." "And when lovely woman stoops to folly,/ She does not invariably come in at four A. M.,/ Singing 'Sweet Adeline'." It would be unjust to identify the poetic efforts of Phyllis McGinley Hayden as "light verse." They are light in the sense that they are easily understood by the untutored reader. But underlying the surface are meanings that are far reaching. They remind readers of the beauty and mystery of life that is so often ignored. They explain to the reader that what at first glance might seem ordinary, is truly, when you look at it properly, is quite extraordinary. W. H. Auden agrees that McGinley's poetry is more than "light": "You could equally call it light verse or marvelous poetry. There is a certain way of writing which one calls light, but underneath it can carry a great depth of emotion."

The June 18, 1965, issue of *Time* features Phyllis McGinley on the cover. Written above is her bio reduced to eight words: "I rise to defend the quite possible She." The "She" was the authentic woman who combined authentic success with domestic tranquility. She did not try to be anything but herself and this is the kind of success we should all seek to emulate.

Phyllis McGinley Hayden passed away in 1978 at the age of 72.

Does a Career Make a Woman Hard?

The issues associated with secular feminism have a long history. In 1848 at Seneca Falls, New York, in a Declaration of Sentiments, a group of feminists made the following statement: "The history of mankind is a history of repeated injuries and usurpations on the part of man toward woman, having as direct object the establishment of absolute tyranny over her."

Women decided to fight back. But their platform was defective. Their narrow view of history was a travesty of justice. Placing all men in a stereotype was exactly the kind of tactic that feminists abhorred. They were launching a movement that was built on a contradiction. By employing a strategy normally associated with men, they were seeking to imitate what they denounced. Men were the enemies not the allies. Feminists were called to arms, to throw off the yoke of tyranny.

A little more than one hundred years later, in 1957, Bishop Fulton J. Sheen wrote a lengthy article encapsulated by a daring title: "Does a Business Career Harden a Woman?" He concluded that, "It is not a question of whether woman should appear in public or be content to reign in private; the question is rather whether she will exercise her role in a specifically feminine way. All the professions can be bettered through her spiritual influence." The Venerable bishop may be excused for bifurcating woman into public and private, for his point is that the career world will not harden a woman but draw benefits from her as long as she is true to her original nature. Thus, Sheen distinguished between woman's authentic nature as feminine and her deviation from that as being a feminist.

The *Book of Genesis* teaches that God created woman from man, whereas man came from slime. He was to be her protector, whereas she was to be his helper, saving him from extremes as the Hebrew word *ezer* indicates. These original roles were twisted out of shape as a result of original sin. Man was not made to be a tyrant, nor was woman made to be at war with him. The sexes were not created to battle each other but to help each other in complementary ways. Secular feminism loses sight of the original vocations of men and women and is fixated on the disturbing effects of original sin.

In 1988, Pope John Paul II turned his attention to the issues of woman in his Apostolic Letter, *Mulieris Dignitatem*. He spoke of the "genius" of woman and "*the fruits of feminine holiness.*" He acknowledged in the Introduction that, "The dignity and the vocation of women [is] a subject of constant human Christian reflection—having gained exceptional prominence in recent years." According to the *Second Vatican Council*, "The hour . . . has come when the vocation of women is being acknowledged in its fullness, the hour in which women acquire in the world an influence, an effect and a power never hitherto achieved. That is why, at the moment when the human race is undergoing so deep a transformation, women imbued with a spirit of the Gospel can do so much to aid humanity in not falling."

Alongside of this outstanding tribute to the dignity and importance of women is a cautionary note. His Holiness warns against 'the 'masculinization' of women." "In the name of liberation from male 'domination,' women must not appropriate to themselves male characteristics contrary to their own feminine 'originality'." There is a well-founded fear that if they take this path, women will not 'reach fulfilment,' but instead will *deform and lose what constitutes their essential richness."*

The Pontiff's words offer a confirmation of what Bishop Sheen had to say about women in the aforementioned article. He is aware that a contradiction cannot lead to a fulfillment. The contradiction to which he is referring is the futile attempt to denounce men and at the same time attempt to imitate them. In the process, women lose their femininity. Abortion, now considered by many as a 'right,' cannot be regarded as being consistent with women's fulfillment. The rejection of men, who are said to be imposing a 'patriarchy' that suppresses women, is also the rejection of an ally that is needed in order for women to achieve their fulfillment.

In 2013 (August 15), *The End of Woman: How Smashing the Patriarchy Has Destroyed Us* was released. Author, Carrie Gless is a Fellow at the Ethics and Public Policy Center and has a doctorate in philosophy from the Catholic University of America. Her central thesis is that feminism does not empower women; it erases them. This unhappy result is brought about by women trying to become something they are not, like the proverbial horse that wanted to sing like a nightingale. Being liberated from one's own original nature is akin to a flower being plucked from its roots.

Dr. Gless reflects on the seeds of contemporary feminism that were planted in the 1800's. She is struck by how many Catholics have embraced secular feminism as if it were congruent with their faith.

It is an odd phenomenon that so many women can become members of a movement that is clearly contrary to scripture as well as to common sense. The Bible portrays women of great strength and leadership. Independence is a myth. We all have a specific nature that was given to us by God. We cannot be independent of ourselves and thrive. Personal authenticity means being true to one's self and not to an ideological group that is bent on overthrowing an imaginary tyrant.

www.ingramcontent.com/pod-product-compliance
Lightning Source LLC
LaVergne TN
LVHW051833080426
835512LV00018B/2858